LIVING BEYOND DISTRACTION

BASED ON A SERIES OF TELECALLS ABOUT
DISTRACTOR IMPLANTS

WITH
GARY M. DOUGLAS AND DR. DAIN HEER

Living Beyond Distraction
Copyright © 2015 Gary M. Douglas and Dr. Dain Heer
ISBN: 978-1-63493-012-3

All rights reserved. No part of this publication may be reproduced, stored in a retrieval system, or transmitted, in any form or by any means, electronic, mechanical, photocopying, recording or otherwise without prior written permission from the publisher.

The author and publisher of the book do not make any claim or guarantee for any physical, mental, emotional, spiritual, or financial result. All products, services and information provided by the author are for general education and entertainment purposes only. The information provided herein is in no way a substitute for medical or other professional advice. In the event you use any of the information contained in this book for yourself, the author and publisher assume no responsibility for your actions.

Published by
Access Consciousness Publishing, LLC
www.accessconsciousnesspublishing.com

Printed in the United States of America

Many thanks to Cheri L. R. Taylor
and Dona Haber
for their contributions in creating this book
out of the transcripts of the
Distractor Implant Telecall Series.

Contents

Chapter One
Anger, Rage, Fury, and Hate 9

Chapter Two
Blame, Shame, Regret, and Guilt 35

Chapter Three
Addictive, Compulsive, Obsessive,
    and Perverted Points of View 67

Chapter Four
Love, Sex, Jealousy, and Peace 95

Chapter Five
Life, Death, Living, and Reality 131

Chapter Six
Fear, Doubt, Business, and Relationship 157

The Access Consciousness Clearing Statement® 183

Other Access Consciousness® Books 187

Access Seminars, Workshops & Classes 189

About Gary M. Douglas & Dr. Dain Heer 193

Foreword

When you find yourself in a situation that you don't seem to be able to change, you may be stuck in a distractor implant.

A distractor implant is something that is energetically entrenched or established in your universe. It is designed to be triggered by the events of your life and to create distractions that keep you from being all that you can truly be and having the life you would truly like to have. They're the reason we believe we have no choice in anything.

The distractor implants are:

- Anger, Rage, Fury and Hate
- Blame, Shame, Regret and Guilt
- Addictive, Compulsive, Obsessive, Perverted Points of View
- Love, Sex, Jealousy, Peace
- Life, Death, Living, Reality
- Fear, Doubt, Business, Relationship

Needless to say, you would be a lot better off without them.

In this book we provide information and seriously effective tools that will enable you to recognize the distractor implants and become free of them.

CHAPTER ONE

ANGER, RAGE, FURY, AND HATE

Gary: Hello everyone, today we're going to talk about the distractor implants anger, rage, fury, and hate. I have invited all of you to send me your questions, and several people have written in asking, "How come I do anger?"

ANGER, POTENCY, AND INTENSITY

Ninety-nine percent of the people in the world do anger as a way of getting control. We have misidentified and misapplied anger as a source of force in the world. We think of it as something that creates a potency.

For many people, *potency* means power or strength, but I'm using it in a slightly different sense. A chemical that can alter other chemicals is considered *potent*. It can be a catalyst to change other chemicals. When you're potent, you can alter everything in your life. You can change whatever is occurring so it works better. As infinite beings, we all have this potency, but often it seems inaccessible to us because it lies beneath distractor implants, which are designed to distract us and keep us from being the infinite beings we truly be.[1]

We tend to misidentify anger as potency because anger gets people to *react*—but it doesn't allow them to *act*.

---

[1] In Access Consciousness®, we often use the word be rather than are to refer to you, the infinite being you truly *be*, as opposed to a contrived point of view about who you think you *are*.

Call Participant: Can you talk about what reaction is?

Gary: Reaction is where x occurs and you do y, whether you want to or not. Something occurs and you react to it rather than being able to act to it.

Call Participant: When we do anger, are we looking for someone else's reaction?

Gary: Yes, you are looking for where you can be in control. That is why you do anger in the first place: you see it as a way of getting control.

Call Participant: Is that true if we are doing anger for potency? When you use potency with us, you are doing it to get a reaction.

Gary: Well, I do force, but I don't do anger.

Most of you do anger rather than force, and unfortunately for almost all of you, you suppress anger. You suppress it and you suppress it—until you react—and then you think that is potency. But that's not necessarily being potent at all. That is creating a situation where you are in reaction and so is everybody else.

Call Participant: Can you explain how you do force?

Gary: I will get very loud. If I want to create a force in your life, I will get very intense with the energy. You have noticed me doing intensity with you. Is it anger?

Call Participant: No.

Gary: No, but it is intensity. The real power in life is the capacity to use intensity when you need to get a point of view across or when you want to get people to do something different from what they are currently doing.

Dain: Here is one of the ways you can tell the difference between intensity and what people call anger: three seconds after you do intensity, you are back to the gentleness of you—or you can be if you choose it. There are no repercussions in your body. There is no elevated heart rate. There's no sense of being stuck in whatever happened. That's not so with anger.

Gary: That's a good point, Dain, because when you do anger from the place of explosion, you are pushing yourself out of true existence into a place of trying to control others. And when you do that, you use a great deal of force against your own body. That's the problem with all distractor implants; they go as a force against your body, which keeps you in a constant state of adrenaline pump at the wrong moments. It means you are in a state of reaction and never in a state of action.

Call Participant: I get anger and potency confused. My father would get angry about everything, even small insignificant things. I get angry too, and sometimes I have a hard time letting go of the anger. I thought I had gotten through this, but recently, I got very angry at a so-called friend. I told her to get out of my life, and when she came near me, I got furious and thought I would hit her!

Gary: When you do anger from the implanted point of view of the distractor implants, you can't let the anger go away because you are in a reactive state. Every time you think about the person, you are in reaction to what they did or what they said that caused you to go off. But what they said or did isn't what caused you to go off. You were triggered by the fact that it was a distractor implant. That's the thing you grew up with. You grew up with somebody who triggered you at every opportunity, and now, given the right circumstance, you must of necessity, go to anger, rage, fury, and hate. This is exactly where you went with your friend.

Dain: We tend to try to understand these things logically, and there is a lot to be gotten from that, but here's something you can do that doesn't involve logic or figuring it out. When you're in middle of whatever is triggering you, say to yourself:

> All the distractor implants creating that I now destroy and uncreate it.
>
> Right and Wrong, Good and Bad, POD and POC, All 9, Shorts, Boys and Beyonds.[2]

---

[2] *Right and Wrong, Good and Bad, POD and POC, All 9, Shorts, Boys and Beyonds* is the Access Consciousness Clearing Statement®. It's short-speak that addresses the energies that are creating the limitations and contractions in your life. When you first read it, it may twist your head around a little bit. That's our intention. It's designed to get your mind out of the picture so you can get to the energy of a situation. For more information about the clearing statement and what the words mean, see The Access Consciousness Clearing Statement at the end of this book.

You'll notice your energy shifting and changing.

These distractor implants keep sticking you. What do I mean by *sticking*? You wanted to let go of the anger, but you were stuck by the distractor implant rather than having the freedom to say, "Hey, get out of my life!" if that was the appropriate thing to say, and then moving on. When you can't move on, you are in the middle of a distractor implant.

Gary: Because you are thinking about this, because you are obsessing about it, you don't have the freedom to choose, or be, or do something different. That is what a distractor implant is designed to do. It gives you no choice.

Dain: You said that when you were a child, your father was always doing anger over trivial, insignificant things. That energy had an intensity to it. You probably misidentified and misapplied that any intensity like that, is this anger, *is* this distractor implant point of view, *is* this stuck place. So when you delivered that energy to your friend, even if it was just an intensity, it was because of the distractor implants you grew up with over the course of your life. You were misidentifying and misapplying that you were doing the same thing you saw happening in your family.

Gary: And you would tend to do the same thing because that is what you learned at the hand of the father.

Call Participant: I am aware that frustration is actually just a lack of information, yet I get frustrated at events and what I think of as human's dumbness—or I go into being right and seeing the other person as wrong. I go so easily into frustration then anger, and I get pissed off about how fast I react. I sometimes surprise myself with the level of energy I have, especially when I have to deal with the same person over and over, like an apartment manager. How do I get over this anger and ask questions?

Gary: That's the place where you say to yourself: "Everything that allows this distractor implant to exist in my universe, I POC and POD it."[3]

---

[3] "POD and POC it" is shorthand for the full clearing statement.

That will give you the place of action. Underneath the distractor implants are all the things that give you power, potency, and the action that puts you, not in charge necessarily, but not at the effect of anybody. It is the place where you have choice. That is the place you've got to get to, the place where you recognize your capacity for choice. Here is a process that came out of my head as a result of reading your questions:

> What physical actualization of the unchangeable and unalterable disease of potency and power are you not acknowledging as the source for the creation of what is hidden beneath all distractor implants? Everything that is times a godzillion, can we destroy and uncreate it all, please? Right and Wrong, Good and Bad, POD and POC, All 9, Shorts, Boys and Beyonds.

ACTION AND REACTION

Call Participant: I have implants in reaction to my husband. Every time he criticizes me, I go to anger. I get angry and I feel insecure. And it seems like every time I get angry, I get heavy metal poisoning.

Gary: First of all, if your husband is telling you that you are a pathetic pile of shit, is that a truth or a lie?

Call Participant: It's a lie, but...

Gary: When somebody tells you something that is not true about you, you will tend to get angry. But instead of reacting with anger, ask some questions:

- What did he mean by that?
- What part of that is loving and caring?
- What part of that is to just be mean to me?

This is the place of not going to anger as a reaction. Asking a question is going to the place of potency and power. The ultimate potency and power is: question, choice, contribution, and possibility.

Dain: If you do what Gary is suggesting, you will be in action, not reaction. This will be true even if what your husband says to you is designed to get you to react. You won't be *reacting;* you will be *acting.*

When you have the dynamic you're describing with somebody, they do things to push your buttons. They're trying to get you to react, and you do react—and the situation goes on the same way for years.

Gary: And it proves that they are right.

Dain: When you change that, when you come out of the reaction and go into action, the other person doesn't get to use that to prove they are right anymore. They may do even more to get you to react, but when you stop reacting, you are no longer at the effect of that situation.

Call Participant: Sometimes it's very hard in the moment, since I have a lot of heavy metal reactions going on. My reaction is caused by the toxicity.

Gary: The toxicity is a result of the distractor implants, because the distractor implants themselves are designed to hurt your body and make it reactive. The body becomes more reactive to the heavy metal programming every time you go into the programming of the distractor implant. That's the reason, whenever you go into anger, you need to run:

> All the anger, all the distractor implants creating this, destroy and uncreate it. Right and Wrong, Good and Bad, POD and POC, All 9, Shorts, Boys and Beyonds.

Think it to yourself. You don't have to say it out loud. Notice how, after you say it two or three times, you suddenly don't have the reaction, and the heavy metals no longer have the same effect on you.

Call Participant: Is anger just anger—or is it always related to an issue? I have anger toward money, family, disease, and other things. When we destroy and uncreate the anger distractor implant, are we destroying and uncreating all of the implants? Or do we have to make a clearing for every issue related to the anger?

Gary: You just clear the distractor implants every time they come up. Pretty soon those will not be issues. They only reason they are issues is that someone issued you this as your problem.

Dain: Be aware of what Gary just said. You have to do the clearing every time anger comes up. A lot of people think, "I POCed and PODed anger once, so it's probably all gone." No, you have to do the clearing every time the anger comes up because there are layers and triggers and all kinds of things that activate it in your world. Every time you POC and POD a distractor implant, you are getting one piece of what activates it.

You need to stay on it, which is why we are doing these calls the way we are, with time between them, so you can POC and POD all the anger, rage, fury, and hate distractor implants as they come up in your life. You are bright enough, brilliant enough, and insane enough to be on this call, and you will perceive a lot more of these things in the world, and they will be a lot easier to deal with because you are getting these tools.

This is how it works. You open yourself to a different awareness of something, you get that awareness in a way you never wanted to know before or in a way that is a lot more dynamic than what you ever thought it could be, but you also get the tools to handle it.

Call Participant: Sometimes when I watch movies about racism or when I perceive something that is really unjust, it makes me very sad and angry.

Hate

Gary: Yes, that's because it takes hate to have prejudice. For prejudice to exist, you have to do hate. Most people don't get that prejudice is always hate. It is never anything less. People create hate in order to create separation. They do it in order to justify the meanness, the anger, the fury, and the rage they are going to do, or might do, or could do, if they needed to do it. Prejudice is just part of the system of anger, rage, fury, and hate, which are some of the primary elements that people on this planet function from.

If there was no hate, would there be the possibility of prejudice and wars and all that kind of stuff? No, because people hate when other people have more money than they do, they hate when somebody has something they don't have. They hate when somebody gets something they think they should have sole access to. These things are ways people create a difficulty that they don't seem willing to overcome. And the reason they can't overcome it is because it is a distractor implant, not reality.

Dain: When you perceive something that is unjust, unnecessary, or inappropriate, and you have sadness or the anger that comes up after the sadness, ask:

- Is this actually anger? Or is this the potency that is required to change this in my life or in the world?
- What other possibilities are available now if I am willing to be the energy of potency?

Call Participant: Is frustration a part of anger? Is it a lesser form of anger?

Gary: The only reason you get frustrated is because you lack information. When you get frustrated, you have to ask: "What information am I missing here that would take care of this?"

I talked with a woman who said she was frustrated. When I told her that frustration happens when you are missing information, she suddenly got the information she was missing. She saw that the people she had been frustrated with wanted to see her as insane, because that made them right. That was really valuable information for her. What freedom do you have when you realize that people have a fixed point of view about you?

Call Participant: I seem to have a lot of frustration.

Gary: Ask: "What additional information do I need here that will make this frustration go away?"

Call Participant: Last week somebody lied to me, and I knew he was lying. I didn't ask if there was a lie, but a surge of potency of energy moved through me. I grabbed something made of stainless steel and started bending it like it was silly putty. What was going on?

Gary: When you recognize that somebody is trying to make you react and you don't, you step into the power and potency that is available to you and you have the ability to do all kinds of things you didn't know you could do.

Dain: Like the grandmother who lifts the car off the grandchild trapped underneath it.

Gary: With one hand.

Dain: If you went beyond all the distractors and distractions from what is true for you, would you have more abilities like that? Probably so. You would probably have more of the capacity you have that has been hidden and sublimated by the distractor implants.

Gary: If you get that most of the people in the world function from distractor implants and live in reaction to everything, and if you stop living in reaction, you have the ability to do things that have never been done before. This is our target—to get you to the place where you can do what has never been done before.

Call Participant: And there was no force used in bending the steel.

Gary: That is the power and potency we have that these implants are designed to keep us from having. They are specifically designed to keep us from having that kind of potency and power.

Call Participant: My emotions have always felt out of control, especially anger and rage. They have dominated my life. I have so much impatience and a fiery temper that wreaks havoc on my nervous system. How much of this is natural to my personality and how much is implanted? How do I handle it all?

Gary: It's all implanted. All of this can be overcome because the level of power and potency that is hidden beneath the distractor implants is what we need to get to and be aware of.

Call Participant: I have a question regarding impatience. Is that a subset of anger? Frequently for me, impatience leads to anger. It is not the same as frustration. It occurs when I am trying to explain something or I when I am waiting for somebody to do something.

Gary: The first problem is that you are a humanoid.[4] The second problem is that you are probably slightly autistic, which means you ask a question, and the other person has already answered it before they speak, and you are ready to move on. They are too slow for you. You start to get angry because you've already gotten your answer. You've already talked back to them in your head and you can't believe they are still carrying on a conversation that's already complete.

Call Participant: Yeah.

Gary: You have to ask: "Am I picking up the whole conversation in my head? Yes? No? Yes! Okay, never mind." Then you won't get that sense of impatience. You will see that you are three steps ahead of everybody in the entire world. It's not a rightness, and it's not a wrongness. It's just a difference in you. You might want to ask: "Am I thirteen steps ahead of this person?"

If you get a yes, you can say, "Okay, I will slow myself down. I'll stop going at the speed of space and I'll go at the speed of a snail or a slug, and I will be fine."

Call Participant: Is that a distractor implant?

Gary: No, that is an awareness you need to have about how you function. You see that the way you function is different from the way other people function. You have to have the awareness of this.

When you get to a place when you feel impatient, there is a ninety-nine percent chance—with all of you—that the reason you are impatient is because you've completed the conversation and the other person is still trying to talk about it. That's like: "I am a little too aware for my britches."

Call Participant: So I just need to slow down and allow everyone to catch up?

---

[4] There are two species of two-legged beings on this planet. We call them humans and humanoids. Humans like to follow the standard pattern. They like to fit in. They don't like change. They don't ask questions. They are in synch with everyone around them. Humanoids take a different approach. They are always asking, "How can we change that? What will make this better? How can we outdo this?" They're the ones who create all the great art, great literature, and great progress on the planet.

Gary: Well, they won't catch up. You just allow them to function at their speed. Just acknowledge it; that will make your life a lot easier.

Call Participant: Could you talk about passive-aggressive behavior? Is that a distractor implant?

Gary: Passive aggressive behavior is just anger, rage, fury, and hate muted. That is all it really is. Some people like to do those things in a very suppressed way. It's anger, rage, fury, and hate, plus fear. It's not anything different than that.

Call Participant: How do distractor implants support holding people's identities in place? And how can we change this?

Gary: Most people think that reaction equals action. For instance, my ex-wife is a person who gets angry all the time. She considers her anger to be her ultimate power, so anger is the one thing she will not let go of. For her, holding on to anger is more important than having a life. She will kill her body with that anger. I recently watched her walking away from me. She looked like she was ten years older than I am when she is actually five years younger.

You are killing your body with the anger you think is so imperative to hold on to. People create themselves, their personalities, and their lives from distractor implants, which is why we are having this conversation. It is why we are doing this call. This stuff is important. It always amazes me when people don't pay attention to it.

Call Participant: Gary, I feel sad about your ex-wife, and how she walked away in that much anger. I had a strong reaction and it made me sad. What's up with that?

Gary: Are you sad for her, sad for me, or sad that someone would kill themselves that way?

Call Participant: It just feels sucky.

Gary: "It's sad" is one thing. "It's sucky" is a judgment. What if it just is what it is? There is so much more available to us, and people do not choose what is greater. Instead they choose what is lesser, as if that is the right thing to choose. You've got to be willing to see what is and get that this is the choice some people make in their lives.

My ex-wife loves her reactive capacities. That is how she identifies as herself, "I am a reaction." It's her way of proving she is who she is. It wouldn't be my way.

Call Participant: I have unexplained anger against my parents from childhood, and I have rebelled against anything they've said or done. It is difficult for me to have a regular conversation with either one of them for five minutes without getting angry or exploding. I have no idea what this is or how to get over it, as I cannot find the reason I get so angry. After I blow up, I start feeling bad for having behaved like that, and it turns into guilt. Can there be anger without a reason?

Gary: Chances are you're experiencing this because you are not looking at past lives. How many past lives have you had with your parents where they were loving to you? Actually that turns out to be a lie, and you are holding on to it anyway. Did you come back to get even with them? How many lifetimes have you had with these people? Did you come back for revenge?

Dain: This is a point of view, but sometimes you come back to get revenge for something that you didn't get revenge for in another lifetime.

Gary: How many past lifetimes do you have with them?

Call Participant: Five is the number I get.

Gary:
> Everything you decided from those lifetimes that is keeping you reactive in this lifetime, will you destroy and uncreate it all? Right and Wrong, Good and Bad, POD and POC, All 9, Shorts, Boys and Beyonds.

Call Participant: If you are willing to overcome anger, and you are POCing and PODing it consciously and regularly, would having your Bars[5] run and focusing on the implant band minimize it?

---

[5] The Bars® are a hands-on Access Consciousness process that involves a light touch upon the head to contact points that correspond to different aspects of one's life.

Gary: You are not supposed to overcome anger. You are supposed to see what anger does. It covers up your power and your potency. So you are not trying to overcome it; you want to POC and POD everything that allows it to hide you from you.

Call Participant: Yes, but it's an implant, right?

Gary: Yes, it's an implant. You have to POC and POD everything that allows that to exist, and pretty soon you won't get angry.

Call Participant: Let's say a client is going through a bitter divorce or a situation where they are blaming someone. Would focusing on the implant band while running Bars help?

Gary: It would be helpful, but if you ask, "How many distractor implants do you have that are keeping that in place?" it might be quicker.

Dain: With the Bars, you are addressing the energy, the thing that is stopping it directly, whereas the implant band handles a lot of long-time considerations.

Gary: You are going to get more results from: "How many distractor implants do you have holding that in place?"

The person will respond, "What do you mean?"

You say, "It's anger, rage, fury, and hate; blame, shame, regret, and guilt. Those are distractor implants. How many distractor implants do you have holding all of this in place so that you are in a constant state of reaction instead of having the ability to move on and act?"

You can't push people to do this. People often try to push others into something different. It doesn't work. An Access facilitator called me yesterday. She had a client who had a portal, and entities were traveling through him all the time. Every time she mentioned "portal," he went psycho on her.

I said, "Don't talk about it. Why mention portals? Just clear the entities and move on." Then I asked, "How much is he paying you for this?"

She said, "Nothing."

I said, "That's why you are not getting results. You are not charging him anything, so he wants to hold on to this so he can see you for free as long as possible. You are kind of cute. That might be why he is coming to you. He wants to get laid." You've got to look at the truth of things, not what you want them to be.

Call Participant: Please give me some tools. I find myself getting angry when my kids start complaining and getting upset.

Gary: Clear all the distractor implants creating the complaints and the upset in that person.

If you have someone who is angry with you, and they are talking with you, say to yourself: "All the distractor implants creating that, POC and POD that." That person will all of a sudden say, "Eh, never mind," and walk away. You can do this when you're talking to someone on the phone, as well.

Call Participant: I am aware that my twenty-four-year-old son is holding anger. I hear him in his room playing video game with others online. He often swears and calls people names. He has always been one to hold on to things. Is there anything I can do to give him more ease?

Gary: Yes, divorce him. You have to destroy and uncreate everything the relationship was yesterday, every day. What will happen with that is that he will start to change. Right now you are trying to help him, and if you are doing "help," you are doing superiority. He hasn't asked for help. You think he needs help, but he doesn't. He is happy with the way he is.

Call Participant: Were we born with distractor implants or did we pick them up?

Gary: We were born with them and we were entrained to certain ones by our family. So is that fun? No.

Call Participant: Any help with rage and anger from severe childhood trauma that has been repressed and forgotten for decades and now the memory is resurfacing?

Gary: The memories are surfacing now because you are starting to recognize the distractor implants and what was holding you back. This is a good sign. Just keep going. Keep running clearings for all the distractor implants, and eventually the awareness and the memories will return. When they do, you will have more freedom.

What you are interested in is more awareness and more freedom; this is the target. We talk about asking questions. The purpose of a question is to give you awareness—not to give you answers. You guys keep looking for answers instead of awareness. So please, start looking for the awareness you get from asking a question, not for the answers you think you are looking for.

Anger, Rage, Fury, and Hate

Call Participant: What is the difference between, anger, rage, fury, and hate?

Gary: *Anger* is the thing that other people use to control you. It's what you use and what you suppress until you explode. This destroys your body. *Rage* is what you get to when you add hate to your anger. Then you get into a rage about it. *Fury* is when you don't hold back. You let go and want to pummel someone to death. *Hate* is a level of loathing of yourself or another that keeps you from having any clarity.

Call Participant: Can you talk about trifold sequencing systems? Are they the same as distractor implants?

Gary: Trifold sequencing systems are a Mobius strip, which means you play an event that happened a long time ago over and over again in your head as though it just happened today. Trifold sequencing systems are basically the source of PTSD.

They are not the same as distractor implants, but they are part of distractor implants in that they are always on a Mobius strip, so you will never get rid of them. To clear them, ask for all the Mobius strips holding the anger, rage, fury, and hate in place. POC and POD every Mobius strip and everything you've resisted and reacted to and aligned and agreed with to allow them to exist.

Dain:
> What physical actualization of the unchangeable and unalterable disease of potency and power are you not acknowledging as the source for the creation of what is hidden beneath all distractor implants? Everything that is times a godzillion, will you destroy and uncreate it all, please? Right and Wrong, Good and Bad, POD and POC, All 9, Shorts, Boys and Beyonds.

Gary: The good news is that having those conversations has made this process more intense.

> What physical actualization of the unchangeable and unalterable disease of potency and power are you not acknowledging as the source for the creation of what is hidden beneath all distractor implants? Everything that is times a godzillion, will you destroy and uncreate, please? Right and Wrong, Good and Bad, POD and POC, All 9, Shorts, Boys and Beyonds.

Dain: By the way, if some of you have noticed that you are feeling distracted, could it be that's the subject we are discussing? Just thought I would point that out for you.

Gary: (Laughing) That was good, Dain!

Dain:
> What physical actualization of the unchangeable and unalterable disease of potency and power are you not acknowledging as the source for the creation of what is hidden beneath all distractor implants? Everything that is times a godzillion, will you destroy and uncreate, please? Right and Wrong, Good and Bad, POD and POC, All 9, Shorts, Boys and Beyonds.

Call Participant: At the end of that clearing, you said, "for the creation of what is hidden beneath all distractor implants," but earlier you said that underneath the distractor implant is the power and potency I desire to be. Can you help me with this?

Dain: Yes, basically, you are what is underneath the distractor implants, but you have made power and potency a disease rather than something you could have with ease.

Gary: It's like you create a disease about potency and power rather than having ease with total potency and power. You use distractor implants to react rather than being the action that could change.

Call Participant: What is the difference between POCing and PODing distractor implants vs. Mobius strips?

Gary: A Mobius strip is an implant too, and when you clear the implants, you start to unlock what allows the Mobius strip to exist and continually play in your head as if it's real.

You take a bigger sweep when you POC and POD the distractor implant. Imagine trying to clean up a big mess with a tiny whiskbroom or a toothbrush. Now imagine taking out a broom and cleaning up the whole mess. With the implants, you take out the big broom. If you do the particles in the Mobius strip, you are doing the toothbrush version.

> What physical actualization of the unchangeable and unalterable disease of potency and power are you not acknowledging as the source for the creation of what is hidden beneath all distractor implants? Everything that is times a godzillion, will you destroy and uncreate, please? Right and Wrong, Good and Bad, POD and POC, All 9, Shorts, Boys and Beyonds.

LIES

Call Participant: I have a question about anger. As we have been talking, I realized that whenever I've had anger come up, I have either subverted it or pushed it down so there would be no acting out of anger in my life. I would sit there and steam or I would leave. When you said that we get angry if there is a lie involved, I looked back and said, "Oh my God! That is what was happening ninety percent of the time. I wasn't angry at what was going on; I was just steaming inside and wanted to leave.

Gary: When you recognize that a lie will create anger and you ask, "Is there a lie here?" you then have the ability to act instead of having the necessity to go away or stuff it. Going away and stuffing it are not actions; those are reactions.

Call Participant: So in that environment, there is just a lie present.

Gary: Well, there may be more than one. If you ask, "Is there a lie here?" you will not buy the lie and you won't create a reaction based on lie. Instead, you will ask, "What is really desired or required here?"

Call Participant: So if I am aware that there is a lie, could I be aware of a lie that is being projected at me—or could I be aware of a lie in my own reality?

Gary: Yes, all of the above and more. Once you acknowledge there is a lie, you have choice. Go back to choice once you acknowledge a lie. If you do not acknowledge a lie, you can't go back to choice.

Call Participant: Acknowledge: "This is a lie," then go back to the four questions?

Gary: Yes, ask:

- What is this?
- What do I do with it?
- Can I change it?
- If so, how do I change it?

Call Participant: I've had a lot of unexplained anger and destructive rage in my life, and I've been abusive with it. It has never made sense to me. I have recently discovered the high antenna I have whenever a lie is present. How much of my abusive anger with me is not being aware of what I was aware of?

Gary: The main thing you have to look at is "How much of this abusive anger is my awareness of a lie?" Ask that question then POC and POD everything you bought and made a distractor implant, because when you find a lie and don't acknowledge it, you tend to put it into the distractor implant universe.

Call Participant: Is that why I could be abusive with me even though it might have been unacknowledged power and potency?

Gary: Yes, you begin with awareness then you go immediately into reaction, because that is what everyone else does. You figure that in order to be like others, you have to do like others.

Anger, Rage, Fury, and Hate

Call Participant: Yeah, and the anger and the rage that I would have was, in my estimation, so ugly and abusive that I would turn that into shame on myself, and then there would be more anger, then...holy shit!

Gary: You are a great distractor implant looking for a place to happen. How about the rest of you?

> Have you been trying to personify yourself as a distractor implant like everyone else is being, doing, and generating? Isn't that nice? Everything that is times a godzillion, will you destroy and uncreate, please? Right and Wrong, Good and Bad, POD and POC, All 9, Shorts, Boys and Beyonds.

Dain:

> What physical actualization of the unchangeable and unalterable disease of potency and power are you not acknowledging as the source for the creation of what is hidden beneath all distractor implants? Everything that is times a godzillion, will you destroy and uncreate, please? Right and Wrong, Good and Bad, POD and POC, All 9, Shorts, Boys and Beyonds.

Gary: Hit 'em again, Dain, hit 'em again.

Dain:

> What physical actualization of the unchangeable and unalterable disease of potency and power are you not acknowledging as the source for the creation of what is hidden beneath all distractor implants? Everything that is times a godzillion, will you destroy and uncreate, please? Right and Wrong, Good and Bad, POD and POC, All 9, Shorts, Boys and Beyonds.

Gary: This is getting heavier. You had better put this on a loop and listen to it nonstop, because you know what? This is the only thing that will get you out from under the crap you have decided is yours.

Dain:

> What physical actualization of the unchangeable and unalterable disease of potency and power are you not acknowledging as the source for the creation of what is hidden beneath all distractor implants? Everything that is times a godzillion, will you destroy

and uncreate, please? Right and Wrong, Good and Bad, POD and POC, All 9, Shorts, Boys and Beyonds.

Call Participant: Does running these loops naturally allow us to be the energy that we need to be when we are communicating to people, because we need to deliver a certain level of potency with our interactions?

Gary: Yes, and the more you become aware of the distractor implants, the more you will realize that if you require this person to react in a certain way, all you need to do is push this button—and you can push that button.

Don't bother doing this with the people in Access, because you are not looking for reaction from them; you are looking for action. But with people who do normal jobs, for instance, when you go to the car rental place, there are people you can get to do blame, shame, regret, and guilt, and they will give you a better car for a lesser price. All you need to do is to have the awareness of how you create the energy of that distractor implant, and all of a sudden they will be doing what you need them to be doing in the way you need them to do it. Now, that is not mean and nasty; it just is being in this reality and making other people function in a way that works for you. In truth, you won't do it with very many people.

When you get to the point when you are not functioning from anger, rage, fury, and hate, because that is the primary distractor implant that runs your life right now, you have the space where you can manipulate and control others as needed, to get a result as needed, based on knowing what's needed.

Call Participant: So the fact that other people are running my life—is that my being unwilling to manipulate other people?

Gary: Yes, and it is also your being unwilling to be active. So instead you are reactive.

Dain: What most of us are handed is that our job is to be reactive. Supposedly it's a lot easier to be reactive, and we are not responsible for the choices we make when we are reactive, so we can blame other people for what happens.

That obviously doesn't work for you, because if it did, you wouldn't be on this call, and in truth, you wouldn't have been attracted to Access Consciousness, because Access is about stepping in and being active in your life, rather than being reactive to this reality and all of its insane whims.

> What physical actualization of the unchangeable and unalterable disease of potency and power are you not acknowledging as the source for the creation of what is hidden beneath all distractor implants? Everything that is times a godzillion, will you destroy and uncreate, please? Right and Wrong, Good and Bad, POD and POC, All 9, Shorts, Boys and Beyonds.

Call Participant: Will you please elaborate on using anger for you generatively to incinerate limitations instead of against you?

Gary: When you are not reactive based on anger and you are, instead, active in relationship to it, you can use anger in a generative way to get people to act rather than react and to do it quickly. It's like the time I saw a kid running out in the street in front of a car. I said, "Stop!"

It was anger and it was also a direction. Suddenly, the kid stopped; he didn't get hit. That was generative anger. That's not because I knew that level of anger was what was needed, but because I had watched his parents use anger against him. I duplicated that anger to get the kid to have an instant reaction to whatever I said.

So that is one way to use generative anger to get something to happen. When you use generative anger, it is really just a pretense of anger. It is not anger, so it has no adverse effect on your body.

Call Participant: I've been using anger to incinerate my limitations by making demands like "This is fucking happening!"

Gary: That's not anger. You don't have to use anger to get that. All you have to do is use the intensity that is the real you.

Call Participant: When I get caught in a distractor implant of anger and I am going to poison myself, is there a clearing I can use to help clear that out?

Dain: If you POC and POD all the distractor implants and destroy and uncreate all that's underneath them, that will change your physiology and the effects of anger in your life, because the effects in your life are based on that implant being in place.

There are three things you want to look at in this anger, rage, fury, and hate area. Three things you want to do in the face of it and they are:

1. POC and POD all the distractor implants. If there is anything else there, and you just had a conversation with someone or it's about some piece of information, ask:
2. What's the lie here, spoken or unspoken? Once you get the lie, your attention will come off it.
3. Who does this belong to? You ask that question because you could be perceiving the anger, rage, fury, and hate that's out there in the world.

Once you've run through the anger, rage, fury, and hate in your life, you should notice most of it has dissipated. Most of it should just be gone, including the adrenaline pump that gets created from it.

Call Participant: I haven't been able to unhook myself today.

Gary: Let me ask you a question: How much of what you are saying you "can't get unhooked from" is your buying something that isn't yours? A lot, a little, or megatons?

Call Participant: Megatons.

Gary:

Everything you've bought and sold yourself and made real for you that actually isn't, will you destroy and uncreate all that please? Right and Wrong, Good and Bad, POD and POC, All 9, Shorts, Boys and Beyonds.

That is blowing a whole lot, so you might actually get free of it. Please know that you all keep buying stuff. For example, when you have parents or siblings who are angry, you tend to try to see the rightness in their point of view. If they are doing anger, rage, fury, and hate, you try to see the rightness in it. You assume they wouldn't do it if they knew what they were doing. No. You've got to acknowledge that it's a distractor implant and they have no idea what they are doing.

You have to get that part, because the majority of the world functions from having no idea what the hell they are doing or why they are doing it, but they keep doing it, thinking they are going to get a different result.

Dain: They don't ever question it, they don't ever think about it, they don't ever think anything different—they just do it because that is what they do. And that's the part you need to get: Ninety-nine percent of the world isn't questioning anything. They've gotten a result with something so they are sticking to it. They may have gotten a result with it once out of a thousand times, but they still stick to it because they got a result with it once.

Call Participant: I recently moved into a new home, and on Friday, Bell Canada was supposed to come and set up my phone. I had to take a day off work and I waited all day for them—but they never came. I was a raging lunatic.

I asked myself, "Who and what are you being? Who are you mad at?" What I got was I was in a rage with myself. I was going to the wrongness of me and how unaware I am. Does that rage keep me in the wrongness of me? The energy of it is huge. Is it mine or someone else's? What would it take to not go to the wrongness of me? Or what would it take to not be a raging lunatic?

Gary: If you start to go to rage, you are in distractor implants. So ask:

> Everything I've done to create this, will I destroy and uncreate it all? Right and Wrong, Good and Bad, POD and POC, All 9, Shorts, Boys and Beyonds.

Once you get to an awareness that what you're doing isn't necessary and you don't have to function from it, a whole new world can show up for you that wouldn't show up for anybody else. But you've got to be willing to ask a question. Getting angry at utility companies is about as fruitless as getting angry at the government.

Call Participant: What's the question I have to ask?

Gary: Will they actually deliver what they say they will? Ninety-nine percent of the time, the answer is no. When you have somebody who is scheduling you for something like that, ask:

- Truth, when will this happen?
- When exactly will this happen?
- Can you give me the exact time?

Tell them it's going to cost you $2000 to do this because you are going to miss something very important, and you need to know more exactly when it's going to happen.

Call Participant: When a woman is pregnant and she gets a contraction or when she gets a menstrual pain, it's normal, and you say, "Oh, this is a contraction" or "This is menstrual!" Rage is like that for me. When it shows up, I know exactly what it is.

Dain: (Said with intensity) POC and POD it. It's a distractor implant. Don't make me go medieval on your ass. POC and POD that shit! That's what the last hour and half has been about. That's what you do. Did you get that energy? That's an example of intensity. That is possible when you function with no distractor implants as your reality. Now that you've experienced it, you won't forget it.

Gary: And you might actually get over rage, but probably not—because it is so much fun.

Call Participant: Thank you.

Dain: I hope you enjoyed this call, and I hope you allow yourself for the next few weeks to use those three things:

1. POC and POD the distractor implants.
2. Ask: Is there a lie, spoken or unspoken?
3. Ask: Who does this belong to? And POC and POD everything that is not yours that holds it in place.

If you do this, hopefully in the next couple of weeks, you will actually get free of these things.

Gary: We'd like you to be free of them, we would like you to be the action you can be in the world instead of the reaction you've been trying to be.

Call Participant: We have a lot of these to do, and I don't have time to go through them during the day, so I have been sleeping with the processes on a loop. Does it work if I have them muted or very low?

Gary: Totally and completely.

Dain: Quite well, actually.

Gary: That is taking full advantage of all the hours in the day. Enjoying your day and taking the evening to POC and POD all these things.

Dain: Thanks everyone. Bye for now.

Chapter Two
Blame, Shame, Regret, and Guilt

Gary: Hello everyone. Today we're going to talk about the blame, shame, regret, and guilt distractor implants. These distractor implants are designed to take away everything that is powerful about you.

In the last call, we talked about anger, rage, fury, and hate and how, through these, you get yourself into a place of reaction and lose the ability to act. With blame, shame, regret, and guilt, you go into a place of judgment where you cannot act. You become reactive. You don't ever act totally and you always, instantaneously, assume a wrongness. This is not in your best interest.

Call Participant: Can you speak about distractor implants and all the ways we take on somebody else's universe?

Gary: We have entrained ourselves to be in synch with everybody else. In this reality, we think being in synch is more important than anything else. How many of you have had the feeling that somehow you are not marching to the same drummer as everyone else?

Call Participant: I chose a Jewish family in this life. Can you please do a clearing on this type of heritage, where the guilt, shame, blame thing seems to be epidemic?

Humans and Humanoids

Gary: Pretty much all churches, cults, and religions are designed to put you into blame, shame, regret, and guilt as often as possible.

The interesting part about this is that it works really well on humanoids—because they will go into judgment of themselves. Humans, on the other hand, do not judge themselves. They tend not to do guilt. Humans will go to blame. They'll say, "I couldn't help myself. You made me do it." They blame you. Humans will always tell you how you're wrong and they're right.

Dain: Blame, shame, regret, and guilt only work on humanoids; they only work against humanoids. So if you're a humanoid, you will always have humans who blame you, refuse to take any responsibility, and try to shame you. They will try to get you to go into regret and to feel guilty while never experiencing those things themselves.

From the human point of view, blame, shame, regret, and guilt are a great humanoid equalizer. They bring humanoids down to the human level, because when you are functioning from blame, shame, regret, and guilt, you are always functioning as less than you. These distractor implants are a way of making you, a humanoid, fit in with the humans—they're a way of making you fit into this reality so you can be controlled by the humans.

Gary: The distractor implants are designed to synchronize you into the human reality, and once you get distractor implants out of the way, you start to have the power and potency of you as a humanoid.

Call Participant: Being aware of the distractor implants and all the trigger systems that allow them to exist and control me—and being able to choose the potency that is underneath them—has changed my reality and allowed me to have more energy than I knew was possible. The deep underlying exhaustion in my body and being that I have been aware of for years has dissipated and all the potency underneath it is now being used generatively.

Dain: This is why we are doing each of these distractor implants in sets of four. Each set of them requires a certain amount of energy to keep it in existence.

Gary:
   How much energy are you using to keep blame, shame, regret, and guilt as real for you? A lot, a little, or megatons? Everything that is times a godzillion, will you destroy and uncreate it all? Right

and Wrong, Good and Bad, POD and POC, All 9, Shorts, Boys and Beyonds.

Call Participant: Are blame, shame, regret, and guilt always directed at me? Are they solely directed at me? Is that correct?

Gary: No, people will blame you, and you will blame yourself.

Dain: Blaming doesn't actually work with humans, but you can blame humanoids by saying something like, "It was your fault. You made me do it."

Call Participant: It seems to me that I only blame myself. I only have shame for my body and me. I don't have shame for anybody else but me. That is what I mean. I don't do it to anybody else. I only do it to me.

Gary: Yes, you are correct. It is designed to interiorize you. It always makes you see you as a wrongness.

> What physical actualization of the self-abusive, interiorizing, self-flagellating, self-mutilating, self-abasing disease of blame, shame, regret, and guilt are you not acknowledging as the source for elimination of being in favor of the wrongness of you? Everything that is times a godzillion, will you destroy and uncreate it all, please? Right and Wrong, Good and Bad, POD and POC, All 9, Shorts, Boys and Beyonds.

THE BODY

Call Participant: I've been extensively gifting and receiving body processes, and each time I do this, it unlocks more of this stuff. Even though you can POC and POD these distractor implants, I am not sure you can get to everything without also doing the body processes.

Gary: That was the reason we set up the body class. We noticed that we could do a lot of POCing and PODing, but unless the body got its share of what it needed, it couldn't get to freedom. The body is an integral part of becoming all of you. It's about becoming who you are. That is the reason we created the body processes.

Call Participant: Unlocking this stuff has been the number one priority in my life, and I am starting to recognize myself for the first time ever. So thank you.

Gary: Thank you. Just know that if you do MTVSS[6] on the crown and perineum, you are likely to get a huge change from doing these distractor implants.

Dain: MTVSS unlocks things at a different energetic level than verbal processing. For a long time, we've been saying that MTVSS unlocks the blueprint of your body. Part of what has occurred is that we have been "printed" into this reality using distractor implants. If you haven't yet taken the body class, I highly recommend that you do so. You'll learn to do MTVSS and many other wonderful body processes.

So many people who have done the body class have said, "I never thought this was possible! I never thought this could exist! I never thought this piece of what I could be could show up!" So many things were unlocked for them in doing these processes. Let that be in your awareness, because those body processes change things from a totally different place than the verbal processing.

Call Participant: You mentioned the impact of distractor implants on the body. Do certain ones affect the body differently than others?

Gary: Not necessarily, but all of them affect the body in one way or another, because you lock them into the body by allowing them to be more potent than you. It's because all these things are a Mobius strip that gets played back continuously, so you can never get out of the automatic playback system of this reality.

Guilt

Call Participant: What is the best way to eradicate, for good, the pervasive feeling of guilt whenever I have some spare time for me?

Gary: Well, first of all, it's not that you have spare time for you. There is no such thing as spare time. It's that you feel guilty for not doing

---

[6] MTVSS (Molecular Valence Sloughing System) is a gentle, deeply relaxing Access Consciousness body process that involves a light touch.

something you have decided you're not going to do when you take time for you. That is one of the reasons guilt is in there. It's to make you feel that you never have value, so you never get to be you. You have to be somebody else.

Dain:
> What physical actualization of the self-abusive, interiorizing, self-flagellating, self-mutilating, self-abasing disease of blame, shame, regret, and guilt are you not acknowledging as the source for elimination of being in favor of the wrongness of you? Everything that is times a godzillion, will you destroy and uncreate it all, please? Right and Wrong, Good and Bad, POD and POC, All 9, Shorts, Boys and Beyonds.

Call Participant: Gary, I have no idea what half of those words mean. Can you go over them, please?

Gary: *Interiorizing* is where you look inside yourself to see where you are wrong. It's where you go to "Oh, I shouldn't have done this. I am ashamed. I have shame in my body. I am guilt ridden. I am bad."

Self-abasement is similar. It's where you say, "Oh, I am a terrible person. I am so wrong." It creates a lot of religious fervor for people, and they go into self-flagellation. *Self-flagellation* is what the guy in *The Da Vinci Code* did. He beat himself and put a cilice around his leg to create pain. Those things are based on the idea that there is a basic, innate wrongness in you. These are ways to make you closer to God by not being everything that you have done wrong. But what if there was nothing innately wrong with you?

Dain: These are things that create the sense that there is an innate wrongness in you, and people can use them to trigger that in you, so you go to that point of view continuously, over and over and over. Particular energies can trigger them.

Call Participant: Since the last call, I have a sense that there is a "me" underneath all this. There is the distractor implant and now there is a "me" as well.

Gary: I used to tell people about distractor implants, and I'd say, "If you are reacting to these implants, it is not really you."

I assumed people would say, "Oh! That's not me. It's a distractor implant," and not buy it, but I assumed wrongly. (Assumption makes an ass out of you and me.) But people do buy it because it is so engrained and synchronized. It's like synchronized swimming, where everybody uses their arms in the same way at exactly the same time. Or it's like line dancing. Everyone is doing the same steps as though they are getting someplace, but they are not getting any place. They are all just dancing to the same tune.

That's the problem. It's like you are some kind of marionette. You have no choice. Blame, shame, regret, and guilt take away choice. That's why we are doing this call. Somehow people either a) don't get it or b) don't realize they actually have choice as to whether they chose to have this problem or not.

Call Participant: Is it that I've given up choice? Like I said, I have a sense of "me" now and "me" before, and I have all these distractor implants there.

BEING VS. THE NEED TO DO

Gary: Yes, but you see we are talking about *being*. Are you encouraged to be in this reality or are you encouraged to *do*?

Call Participant: To do.

Gary: Yes, and with these distractor implants it's like this:

- Blame—You did it wrong.
- Shame—I did it wrong.
- Regret—I shouldn't have done it.
- Guilt—How could I do such a terrible thing?

All of those are places where *doing* becomes greater than *being*. If you start to realize that these distractor implants keep you from being, you can start to get that the being is underneath them. It is what is hidden beneath the distractor implants.

The first set, anger, rage, fury, and hate, was about the potency and the power. This set, blame, shame, regret, and guilt, is about the being.

Call Participant: It's like you don't even know they're ruling your life.

Gary: Yes, they rule your life. That's the most important thing you said. There are a thousand ways in which you have given up being in control of your life and being able to rule your own life. You have no capacity to do anything but react to a situation or react to a set of circumstances with specific responses.

Dain: The distractor implants take you out of a set of responses that you as a being would have, and they put you into responses that tie you back into this reality. Where something could expand you beyond this reality, these implants loop back and tie your threads into this reality so you are always contributing to it rather than contributing to undoing or unlocking it.

> What physical actualization of the self-abusive, interiorizing, self-flagellating, self-mutilating, self-abasing disease of blame, shame, regret, and guilt, are you not acknowledging as the source for the elimination of being in favor of the wrongness of you? Everything that is times a godzillion, will you destroy and uncreate it, please? Right and Wrong, Good and Bad, POD and POC, All 9, Shorts, Boys and Beyonds.

Gary: "The need to do" should be added at the end of the process.

Dain:
> What physical actualization of the self-abusive, interiorizing, self-flagellating, self-mutilating, self-abasing disease of blame, shame, regret, and guilt, are you not acknowledging as the source for the elimination of being in favor of the wrongness of you and the need to do? Everything that is times a godzillion, will you destroy and uncreate it, please? Right and Wrong, Good and Bad, POD and POC, All 9, Shorts, Boys and Beyonds.

Gary: Wow!

Call Participant: As you were doing the clearing statement, the term self-eradication is coming up.

Gary: When you look at *doing* instead of *being*, that is eradication of being. This whole area is designed to eradicate your being in favor of the rightness of doing something that is wrong in order to prove that you are wrong. So ultimately, it is eradication of self in every respect, and you show up with the sense that you are invisible and unseen.

Call Participant: How can you tell whether something is stemming from a distractor implant or an entity?

Gary: The only way to tell whether it's an entity (and usually it isn't—usually it's an automatic reaction) is if you hear the word "you" in your head: "You are bad. You did it wrong. You're to blame." It's the entity's way of controlling you. Entities only use distractor implants as a system for controlling you.

Dain: You would always say "I." If you hear "you" in your head or "you" in what you are thinking, referring to yourself, that's an entity. If you hear "you," know that it ain't *you*. It's an entity.

Power and Potency

Call Participant: Since the last call about anger, I seem to be experiencing more anger than ever before in my life, especially in the last few days. I've been running the clearings and doing the POCing, and PODing, but it seems like pinpricks in the hide of an elephant. It doesn't seem to be shifting very much.

Gary: If you are doing anger, rage, fury, and hate, and you have, blame, shame, regret, and guilt for the fact that you have been angry on top of that, you learn with great intensity how to punish yourself by suppressing your anger at all times. The fact that the anger is increasing probably indicates that you are moving into this next implant, which is one of the ways you make yourself wrong for every choice you make.

Dain: On the last call, we talked about the idea that anger is actually potency with the distractor in place. So when we suppress the anger distractor implant, we also suppress the potency.

And the thing about blame, shame, regret, and guilt is the way many of you make it the wrongness of you.

Recently Gary and I were sitting at dinner, talking. As a result of different choices he and I have made, things are showing up a lot differently and there are many possibilities available to us, yet I was going to a place I had learned to come from, which was: "What am I not doing yet? What's not going on? What should be going on that isn't?"

Gary said, "That's part of the blame, shame, and regret of things. Why don't you ask: "What's the possibility here that I haven't yet chosen, or embraced, or acknowledged?"

Gary: It's really important for you to start acknowledging this. You probably don't recognize it, but you have a lot of power and potency. The fact that you are getting to anger is a good sign, not a bad sign.

You've got to ask: "Am I using anger to control people? Or am I angry because this person is pissing me off and I know it doesn't have to be this way?"

Call Participant: Yes, I can see the potency beneath the anger, but I...

Gary: You are not asking: "Am I doing potency or anger here?" The energy of potency and anger are very similar. But they are not the same.

Dain: They are extremely similar, but there is a freedom and a space in potency that is not there with anger.

Gary: So start asking: "Am I doing potency or anger here?" Dain used to say, "I am so angry about this," and I would always laugh.

Dain: Which, I have to say, doesn't make you any less angry when you think you are angry.

Gary: I would start to laugh, because I realized it had nothing to do with anger. It was always his potency showing up. So I would laugh, and Dain would get angrier, and I would say, "Good potency, dude!"

Dain would say, "Argh, you are so frigging infuriating!" and I'd say, "Yeah, I know! Isn't it fun?"

You are very potent, and when you have potency to the degree that most of you do, you are going to find that energy will come up. You've got to ask: "Is this potency or anger?" The difference between the way potency and anger feel is very slight, but there is a difference. That is how the distractor implant was put in. The anger was close enough to your potency to attach this other stuff to it. The same thing applies with the doing and the being. That is why these things are so insidious and invidious.

Call Participant: Does potency need to be channeled in some way?

Gary: No, it just needs to be acknowledged to start with. You will learn to channel it later. Learn to acknowledge it first, and you can learn to use it later.

Call Participant: Sometimes, I get an awareness of things unraveling in my body and in my awareness. The potency is coming through more and more. Sometimes it seems like there's a mix between the trigger system of the distractor implants and potency at the same time.

Gary: That's how distractor implants were created. In order to have an implant of any kind, you either have to align and agree with something or you have to resist and react to something. You may not have been resisting and reacting to these things, but you were aligning and agreeing with your potency—and there is such a close connection between potency and anger. The alignment and agreement with your potency was the component that was necessary to induce this implant electronically into your field.

Call Participant: What do you mean by "aligning and agreeing with my potency"?

Gary: When you are truly potent, you say, "Hey, I am so powerful!" That's alignment and agreement with your power.

We are trying to unlock all of this so you have a different way of being in the world, a different way of doing in the world, and a different way of functioning that will allow you the power and the potency and all the elements of it.

Call Participant: Do I have a confusion about being and doing?

Gary: We all have a confusion about being and doing because we've been taught that we have to *do* to prove that we *be*. But you don't have to do to prove that you *be*, because if you are *being*, you have a lot of *doing* you do. And when you do something, you get it done in a heartbeat. For example, I've been packing up a container of antiques to send to Australia. It's a huge job. Brendon came over to help me and in two days, we got it all accomplished. I had a screen I was going to send, and the back of it needed to be upholstered. I took it to the upholstery shop at ten in the morning and got it back at six o'clock that evening. Done! Upholsterers don't do that.

When you are being you, everything in the world aligns and agrees with allowing you to have things happen instantaneously. This happens more and more—not less and less. When you walk out of *doing* into the place of being able to *be,* things happen instantaneously and with ease.

Every one of these distractors, blame, shame, regret, and guilt, are about "I did it wrong. I shouldn't have done it." It's *doing* from the wrongness point of view. Being in choice is a completely different universe. It changes the way you function in life. We are trying to get you to the place where you can be you and whatever you do happens with such ease and such joy that you feel like you are not really doing anything. You feel like you are standing still and everybody else sees you moving at the speed of space.

Call Participant: Do we do *instead of* choosing? *And if we* choose, do *we actually have to* do?

Gary: You just went into the distractor implant "I don't have to do."

Call Participant: Explain that, please.

Gary: If you are *being,* then *doing* is just part of *being.* It's just one of the many choices you have available to you. You are thinking that *doing* is something you don't want to do. You're thinking you want to *choose* so that *doing* will just happen. It's not quite that way. What you're describing is alignment and agreement with the idea that *being* doesn't require you to *do*—and that allows the implant to be attached to you.

Call Participant: I am getting it, Gary. Thank you. I will be listening to this twenty-five million times.

Interesting Point of View

Dain: That's what the tool "Interesting point of view, I have this point of view" eliminates. If you were to do that for six months, you'd be free. Every one of these distractors functions from a limitation where you have aligned and agreed with something or resisted and reacted to something, which means you are not being "interesting point of view."

With "interesting point of view, I have this point of view" *being* gets so much easier. As Gary pointed out, there is a hairsbreadth difference between anger and potency. And if you are willing to be an "interesting point of view," your potency is increasing. And you can't get stuck in the distractor implant of anger as your potency increases.

That's why we introduce "interesting point of view" and being in allowance in the very beginning of Access Consciousness. When you're in allowance, you don't align and agree nor do you resist and react. Everything is just an interesting point of view. We're trying to get people to a place where they can be unaffected by everything that is a limited point of view.

Call Participant: So if we go into "interesting point of view," we are not going into alignment and agreement even of the positive?

Gary: Exactly.

Call Participant: Thank you.

Call Participant: When you talk about aligning with my potency, it makes me sad. I was acknowledging my potency, which is something that I really like, something I had created or chosen, and something that was cool about my life, and then I destroyed that immediately after I had acknowledged it.

Gary: What's wrong with destroying?

Call Participant: It's not fun—and I would like to shift that.

Gary: You've got to acknowledge what you are good at and then destroy anything that creates it as a limitation. If you say, "Oh, this is so wonderful!" you end up creating it as a limitation of what you can have. Instead of "This is so wonderful!" it's "Oh, it's so interesting, I have that capacity. Cool. What else have I got?"

Dain: There's a temptation to try to stay in one place.

Gary: Wait a minute! I just got something. The *liking* of it makes it a *doing* instead of a *being*. "I like that so much about me" is a conclusion. If you do it as an interesting point of view, you ask: "And what else do I have available?" It goes to question instead of the conclusion, "I like that about me," which turns it into a doing.

Call Participant: I just said, "That's cool, what else is possible?" That's why I was confused that the destruction part showed up.

Gary: What about: "That's cool. I can destroy that too, and what else can I create that's even greater?"

Call Participant: (Laughing) So I can ask, "What else can I create that would be fun too?"

Gary: Yes. "What would be even greater and more fun than this?"

Dain: It's got to be a constant state of forward movement that comes from being in the question. Otherwise, you will fall back to the lowest common denominator of this reality, which is where distractor implants and everything that is heavy and that you don't like about this reality lives.

There is a tendency to think, "The antidote to hating myself forever is going to be to liking this thing about me." No, that's not it. I know Access facilitators who used to say that. They would say, "This keeps causing a catch in my world." I realized it was because they were trying to use a positive polarity to undo a negative polarity that they were functioning from—which is this reality's point of view.

The key is to move forward without the polarity. To do that use:

- Interesting point of view, I have this point of view.
- What else can I create that's even greater than this?

Gary: Yes, then you can move without the polarity.

Call Participant: Brilliant.

Call Participant: I am a trainer and speaker and I love what I do. I've never had to work very much in my life, and there has always been a part of me that doesn't like to work. I like to play. I am wondering...

Gary: So as somebody who is truly *being*, *doing* is play for you. You have that part right. That is how you can make money. Ask: "What can I play at today, that will make me money right away?"

Call Participant: I have always felt that something is there that keeps me away from doing that or being that.

Gary: Notice you said *doing* which is the distractor implant. Whenever you go into the *doing* point of view, blame, shame, regret, and guilt are going on. You have shame about the fact that you don't like to work. You have blame about the fact that you have to work. You have regret about the fact that you don't make money correctly. And you have guilt that you are still out there struggling. All of those are about doing, aren't they?

Call Participant: Yes.

Gary: *Being* is the source for the creation of doing play with everything, and when you start to play with everything, you can create and generate constantly. *Being* is the source of generation. *Being* is the source of creation. *Being*, when done with play, is choosing how you are playing today to determine what you would like to create right now.

Call Participant: I would like to share my experience during the last week. I used to be very angry at my husband. I POCed and PODed the anger every time it came up, and it worked like a charm. But now my husband is getting angry! He is getting more and more intense; he has gotten to the point of being abusive. I am not angry now—but I run away when he is. What does that mean? Why does he get angry when I am not getting angry?

Gary: He has to go to anger to try to control you now because the old system doesn't work anymore.

Dain: He is trying to maintain the old system that you just changed. Here's what you can do: When he gets angry, POC and POD all the anger, rage, fury, and hate; all the blame, shame, regret, and guilt; and all the distractor implants in his world.

Gary: Do it silently.

Dain: Yeah, not out loud or he'll punch you in the face.

Call Participant: Sometimes, it is so intense that I run away. It's too much for my comfort.

Gary: Don't run away. Stand and push the barriers down so that he has nothing to punch at. Do not let the energy come to you. Push the barriers down and pull the energy *through* you.

Dain: This is something Gary had to do personally because his ex-wife was an anger monster. He got the information that the way to handle this was to simply stand there and lower all his barriers and pull the energy through him like crazy.

Before he started to do this, she would rail and yell at him for forty-five minutes until she finally succeeded in breaking his barriers down, and then she'd get over it in three minutes. This is something he's got personal experience with.

Gary: I have lots of personal experience with this one, let me tell you. It's not fun.

Call Participant: Is running away reaction instead of potency?

Gary: Yes, it's a reaction when you try to run away. It's as if you are trying to create a barrier that he can't get through. Don't create barriers. That's aligning and agreeing with the anger, which activates the implant again. You've got to sit there, push the barriers down, and allow the energy to go through you. When you do this, he will run out of steam in a heartbeat! He'll end up laughing at the end of it because he'll feel foolish.

Call Participant: Thank you so much.

Gary: You are welcome. Dain, let's run that process again.

Dain:
What physical actualization of the self-abusive, interiorizing, self-flagellating, self -mutilating, self-abasing disease of blame, shame, regret, and guilt are you not acknowledging as the source for the elimination of being in favor of the wrongness of you and

the need to do? Everything that is times a godzillion, will you destroy and uncreate it, please? Right and Wrong, Good and Bad, POD and POC, All 9, Shorts, Boys and Beyonds.

Regarding the need to do, how much of the doing that you do is trying to undo this pervasive feeling, this energy of blame, shame, regret, and guilt that you perceived in you and around you and that you thought was you your whole life?

Gary: Even if it wasn't yours.

Dain:
> Everything that is times a godzillion, will you destroy and uncreate it, please? Right and Wrong, Good and Bad, POD and POC, All 9, Shorts, Boys and Beyonds.

Call Participant: This weekend, I rented a venue for a class, and it got damaged by some of the kids who were there. The organization that owned the venue said it didn't want to rent it to me again. I went to my old default position of having a tightness in my belly, feeling guilty and uncomfortable, and wanting to figure out how to fix it. I recognized what I was doing, and I cleared the distractor implants around that. I said, "Wow, that's a lot of potency that I lock in my body."

Gary: Hold on, just a second. Is it you that you lock it *in* your body or that you lock it *out* of your body?

Call Participant: I lock it out of my body, absolutely, but I experience the locking out of my body in my body. I recognized that when I was willing to not indulge in the guilt, I could manipulate the situation. It didn't necessarily sound any different—it was still "I am so sorry. What can I do to make up for the damage I've done?" and all that stuff—but there was a play and a lightness to it. I didn't go into the wrongness of me. It was such a different experience. And my body didn't contract like it did in the past.

Gary: Excellent. Funny, you just answered the question I was about to read:

Call Participant: How would you use the blame, shame, regret, and guilt, assigned to you to your advantage?

Gary: You would say, "I am so sorry. I had no idea that was going to happen. What can I do to make up for the damage done? Please tell me! I am a terrible person and I will do anything I can to make it up to you!" That's an example of using the situation to your advantage, because most people would go into blame, shame, regret, and guilt.

When you do that, the other person will go into guilt. They'll say, "Oh, she is actually a nice person," which is guilt. Then they'll go into regret: "I am being way too tough on her." They'll go from saying, "You are a terrible person, and we are never going to let you rent this venue again" to "You are really a nice person, and we know you didn't do it intentionally, so we are going to back off our point of view."

Call Participant: I feel like I am aware of a window so I will be able to rent this venue again in the future. I wouldn't necessarily have been aware of that window if I had indulged in guilt.

Gary: Exactly, that's why it's imperative to get over this, folks.

Dain: There wouldn't have been a window if you had indulged in the guilt, because your distractor implant would have played the other half of something they were aligning and agreeing with or resisting and reacting to. You would have created a lockdown situation in which neither of you were free.

You would have been stuck together by your alignment and agreement and your resistance and reaction; like two poles of a magnet. This is an example of what distractor implants create, and when you use the tools we're giving you on this call as well as the body processes, all of a sudden, you are different. All the stuff that used to trigger you isn't there anymore. You cease to become the effect of these different kinds of polarities.

Gary: Wherever you align and agreed with a point of view, or resist and react to a point of view, you lock yourself up. If you had gone into guilt and "I can't believe you are doing this to me," they would have thought of you forever, and you would have thought of them forever. Which means, where is your energy going? To the past? To the present? To the future? Or into a non-existent universe? It would be going into a non-existent universe.

Call Participant: Gary, can you talk a little bit more about locking that outside of my body?

Gary: When you have those reactions, the reactions are the sensory awareness your body is trying to give you of the distractor implants and how they are affecting you. If you don't get that you are locking the potency out of your body, you don't have choice and you don't have action. You only have reaction, which is what every distractor implant is designed to create. They are designed to put you into total reaction, not into action at all.

Call Participant: Are you saying that our body is telling us when we have something going on inside it, that the body is advising us or showing us "Hey, this distractor implant is affecting you. Look at it."

Gary: Yeah.

Call Participant: So pay attention, right?

Dain: Do you see how brilliant that is? If you get only that from this call, if you truly get that your body is telling you that something is going on, you see that you have to be a detective. This is what you learn in Access Consciousness by asking questions like "Okay, what is this going on?"

Then you can say, "Body, thank you so much for letting me know that my head is buried in a pile of poo." Our bodies continually tell us when something is going on. Your body is saying, "I am letting you know what you are creating as your frigging life! And you, dummy, have been asking to change it, but you never listen to me. Here you are, you dummy, trying to act like you are conscious."

I just want to speak on behalf of your body for a moment. Please stop making your body wrong for what it's showing you, what it's sharing with you, and what it's telling you about what is going on! It's like your body is bringing you a gift. It's bringing you an amazing gift of possibilities, and you act like it's a cat bringing you a dead bird. What if you could start saying, "Hey body, thank you so much for what you are telling me"? What if you could ask, "What tools can I use here to change this stuff and move forward?"

Blame, Shame, Regret, and Guilt

Call Participant: What can I do to rid myself of the despairing, bad-tempered regret I have about the way I have mismanaged money and real estate in the past?

Gary: Stop looking to the past. Blame, shame, regret, and guilt are designed to put you into looking at what you did as a wrongness, so you loop back to the wrongness of you. You continually loop back to the wrongness of you, so you always be the wrongness of you.

Dain:
> That and all the trifold sequencing systems creating it and everything else that holds that in place, will you destroy and uncreate it, please? Right and Wrong, Good and Bad, POD and POC, All 9, Shorts, Boys and Beyonds.

Call Participant: When I started to become aware of distractor implants, I saw them coming from the outside, like society was using them against us. For example, when you talk about sexuality, a lot of people make you feel regret and guilt for choosing someone of the same sex. On this call, it seems like everyone is talking about something within them, but I am looking at how everyone is triggering things from outside of us.

Gary: Distractor implants are designed to trigger on the outside in order to make you interiorize and look into you as the wrongness of you.

Dain: If you didn't have any of these things that could be triggered on the inside, they wouldn't get triggered from the outside.

Gary: We are trying to get the trigger gone. Access is a trigger guard. It's the safety catch on the trigger, so you don't pull it.

Dain: We want to remove all of your big red buttons that say "Push Here to Inferior-ate Me."

Gary: "Push Here To Make Me See Me As Wrong." Let's run the process again. We are going to add something to it.

> What physical actualization of the self-abusive, interiorizing, self-flagellating, self-mutilating, self-abasing disease of blame, shame, regret, and guilt, are you not acknowledging as the source for the

elimination of being, the Mobius strip of the wrongness of you, and the need to *do*? Everything that is times a godzillion, will you destroy and uncreate it, please? Right and Wrong, Good and Bad, POD and POC, All 9, Shorts, Boys and Beyonds.

Call Participant: I often feel guilty that I am not doing what I am supposed to be doing. Is that all distractor implants? Is that the whole "doing" piece you were talking about earlier?

Gary: Yes. If you are always focusing on what you are not doing, you have to feel you are somehow wrong for not *doing* all the time. You are focusing on *doing*; you are not allowing yourself to be what would change it.

Dain: You are also focusing on the past of the not-doing. You're focusing on the past, rather than being present and moving forward.

Call Participant: I sense regret that I was not aware of the Access Consciousness tools when raising my children. What am I distracting myself from?

Gary: Well, first of all, you are distracting yourself from the fact that you are an infinite being who can change everything, including the past. Start with this: "Everything I was to my children yesterday, I now destroy and uncreate it all." If you do that every day, your kids will forget all the things you did to them that you weren't supposed to do to them.

Dain:

> What physical actualization of the self-abusive, interiorizing, self-flagellating, self-mutilating, self-abasing disease of blame, shame, regret, and guilt, are you not acknowledging as the source for the elimination of being, the Mobius strip of the wrongness of you and the need to *do*? Everything that is times a godzillion, will you destroy and uncreate it, please? Right and Wrong, Good and Bad, POD and POC, All 9, Shorts, Boys and Beyonds.

Call Participant: Can you please talk about how, when you buy into one distractor implant, you are in all of them? Is it like the one distractor implant you always buy as your Kryptonite allows the other twenty-three to activate again? How does this work and how can we change it?

Gary: If you are aligning and agreeing with your point of view about your potency, or your being, or anything else, whichever one of those is most easily affected for you is the one that was used as the primary source for the implantation of these distractor implants. It's like all of them can exist because of that particular one, so you have to be willing to recognize that there is a different possibility.

Call Participant: When you say "the one that was used as the primary source," what do you mean by that?

Gary: Let's say potency is the one thing you aligned and agreed with: how powerful you were.

Call Participant: Yes.

Gary: So the thing you are looking for is your potency. That would mean anger, rage, fury, and hate were the easiest to apply, because your potency came across from the anger—the slight difference in anger and potency. So that was the one they were able to use to install all the rest of the distractor implants.

Call Participant: Wow, so how do you concentrate on the anger? I would concentrate on the anger. What would I...

Gary: Nope, nope, nope. You are trying to find the problem and fix the problem. Don't try to fix the problem. Try to be the creator.

Call Participant: What would that look like?

Gary: "What can I create beyond this that nobody has even thought of?"

Dain: And "What physical actualization of the reality that has never existed, am I now capable of generating, creating, and instituting?"

Call Participant: Thank you very much.

Call Participant: You said, "generating, creating, and instituting." What came up for me was "generating, creating, and actualizing." What is the difference between instituting and actualizing in this instance?

Gary: When you generate and you create, you start the actualization. If you start the actualization when you institute it every day and contribute to the platform, it gives you a greater spring board from which to create more.

If you generate and create, you start to actualize; you start to bring into existence what you are asking for. Then you have to institute. You have to do the thing that will expand it every day. That's the institution part.

Call Participant: So are the generation and creation an actualization?

Gary: They're the beginning of actualization. You have to institute it on a daily basis. That puts it into a physical reality in totality.

Call Participant: I always have the point of view that guilt is about what you do, but shame is about who you are. Can you talk about that?

Gary: It doesn't matter how you define it. Shame is about what you are *doing*. Shame is the idea that you did something bad, which is why you shouldn't do it, which is why you should judge you for being such a bad person. You could define that as who you are, but it actually isn't who you are. It's what you've been doing that you are not proud of.

I once did some past life regressions in which I discovered I had been a hired gun and I killed people for money. Then there was one event in that lifetime when I said, "I am never doing this again. This is just not workable!"

It wasn't shame, blame, regret, or guilt. It was "I am not doing this ever again." The idea of killing is not foreign to me nor is it something I would resist. I would kill somebody if that was going to work, but I hate cleaning up the mess.

Call Participant: Let's say in a past life, I was a nun. Wouldn't being a nun be who you are rather than what you do?

Gary: No, it's what you were *doing* in that lifetime to prove that you were *being* a proper, religious person.

Call Participant: Okay, got it. Shame has run incredibly deep for me, and I've always described myself as having a shame core. Is that the implant or is it something…

Gary: That's the implant. Right now look at being proud of something you do. Feel the energy of that, and then feel the energy of shame at the core. They are a similar vibration, which is what allowed you to be implanted with shame—because your pride is the other side of it.

Call Participant: So I use pride to combat the shame?

Gary: Yes. You've tried to be proud of what you do and what you are instead of asking: "What else can I do that I haven't even considered yet?"

Dain: Which opens up options other than trying to be proud or trying to undo the shame. Ask: "What physical actualization of a reality that has never existed am I now capable of generating, creating, and instituting?"

I highly suggest putting that on a loop and running it over, and over, and over again for the next year or so. I've been using it all the time, and it changes things every single time I run it because every moment is a chance to physically actualize a reality that has never existed before. And that's what starts opening up!

Distractor implants make you believe you have one choice or the other. One choice or the other, one choice or the other—and that's not true for you as a being. It's what you've allowed to be true by aligning and agreeing with these things over and over again.

Gary: Let's run that process again.

Dain:
> What physical actualization of the self-abusive, interiorizing, self-flagellating, self-mutilating, self-abasing disease of blame, shame, regret, and guilt are you not acknowledging as the source for the elimination of being, the Mobius strip of the wrongness of you, and the need to do? Everything that is, will you destroy and uncreate it, please? Right and Wrong, Good and Bad, POD and POC, All 9, Shorts, Boys and Beyonds.

Call Participant: In my family, Dad did anger and Mom did (and still does) guilt and shame. Being the aware rebel kid, I've made guilt and shame of me a gut-wrenching situation. POCing and PODing it is not working. I am ashamed of me, of who I am.

Gary: First of all, you are truly ashamed of you? Or do you have pride in the fact that you survived two idiots? All of you might want to look at the fact that you survived the idiots you call your parents. Please know that you have been doing shame and guilt. You've been doing anger. You've been doing these things as though they're a way to come to a sense of pride in self. No. It's about *being* you, not *doing*.

You survived people who did blame, shame, regret, and guilt. You survived all of those. You not only survived—you came out the other side. You're able to look at things in a different way and recognize, "I don't have to be any of this." They did whatever they needed to do in order to get you to do what they thought you should do that would make you better than them. And that's the story.

> Everything that is times a godzillion will you destroy and uncreate it please? Right and Wrong, Good and Bad, Pod and Poc, All 9, Shorts, Boys and Beyonds.

Dain: Some of you only had two idiots, you lucky sons of guns. I had numerous idiots and I also had my mom, who loves me to death.

At one point, I was looking at my situation with my dad and my step-mom, both of whom are humans of magnitude, and both of whom put all kinds of weird stuff on me. I saw that I was resisting anything I could do that would create my life and living. I couldn't be productive; I couldn't be creative and generative.

Gary said, "You need to change your perspective." He asked:

- What gift did you get by being there?
- What greatness do you have that you wouldn't have had otherwise?
- What different point of view do you have about the world that you wouldn't have had?

- And what do you understand about people and their limitations that you can now facilitate others out of as a result of living with these people?

You might ask those questions about your past, your childhood, and the people you've been with. You would not have been with those people just to perpetuate limitation. You've done it in this lifetime so you can be a facilitator of change. How many of you know you are here to contribute to changing the world?

Participants: Absolutely!

Dain: That's why you did it.

Gary: That's why you had those people in your life. That's why those people did what they did.

Dain: There is something you've gained from this. Please start asking:

- What did I gain from this?
- What am I here to do?

It will change your perspective on your reality if you are willing to realize that you did this in order to change the world.

Gary: You had something you wanted to be totally aware of in a cognitive sense in order to help others who have been functioning from the same place.

Dain: And because of something you have, and are, and because of something they have, and are, you knew that putting those two things together, was going to create a particular result that you wanted to create. That's what you need to look for.

Call Participant: Are you talking not only about parents, Dain, but also the abusive situations I put myself in?

Dain: Yes.

Call Participant: Thank you.

Gary: You do those abusive situations because you think you need to have the blame, shame, regret, and guilt. That is entrained in you from the very beginning. You think that you have to align and agree and be in synch with everybody else. You have to march in step at all times. And none of you are very good marchers. You don't march for shit.

Call Participant: I have a physical deformity that I masked as a child. I had to wear special clothing, and I still do now. It is something that people commented on when I was a kid, and still do now. Do I just POC and POD it until it has no effect? Is that really it?

Gary: No, it's more about doing "interesting point of view" and "What did I create with this that I am not acknowledging that gives me a power and potency that I am not claiming?" You never look from there. You look from how it must be a wrongness because you are not in synch with everybody else. It's like "Okay, so what?"

I didn't have a physical deformity; I was deformed mentally. Nobody could see my deformity, but everybody could hear it when I opened my mouth.

Call Participant: Isn't "deformity" in itself a judgment, Gary?

Gary: Yes, it is.

Call Participant: But there are things that fall out of the norm, which people judge as deformity.

Gary: Yes, I understand. That's the reason I say I was deformed in my mental point of view. I was not in the ordinary universe. I did not fit. I did not march in synch with everybody else nor do you. So what did you gain from that, that you haven't acknowledged? There is something you gained.

A lot of people want to feel guilty and shame ridden because they don't have a physical deformity and you do. They think they should be doing stuff for you. Why aren't you using that to your advantage? You can ask, "How can I use these people?" You can say, "Hey, you can give me money because I am deformed!" There are all kinds of things, you can do with this.

A guy who was in a wheelchair came to see me once, and I felt terrible that he was in a wheelchair and I wasn't. I asked, "Can I help you?"

He said, "No, I can take care of myself." This was a different point of view, and I needed to look from a different place.

We were going to lunch. He went down the back steps of the house in his wheelchair. They were the steepest damn steps that I almost tripped going down them. He went down them at the speed of light with the wheelchair tipped up in the air, hit the ground and took off.

He said, "Catch me if you can!"

I said, "It's not fair! You have wheels. You can go faster than me!"

I got that he didn't see his condition as a deformity. He saw his condition as a difference, and it gave him places where he could use it to his advantage. You have to look at where you can use how you are "deformed." The "deformity" might be your race, color, or creed; it could be part of your blame, shame, regret, and guilt; it could be a mental deformity or a physical deformity. With all of these, you want to ask: "How do I use this to create something greater?" And you can use the distractor implants to get people to do everything for you.

Call Participant: I have a question about dealing with people who sleep walk through life. I am not willing to validate anyone else's reality when it's a lie.

Gary: If you are not willing to validate someone's reality, you're being mean.

Call Participant: So what is your suggestion?

Gary: Acknowledge their reality as their reality. It's an interesting point of view. You wouldn't want to live like that, but it's their choice. When you won't validate someone's reality, it's like putting up your dukes and saying, "Fight, asshole!"

Call Participant: How do you have a conversation with someone when they are invested in their trauma and drama? What do you say?

Gary: You say, "If I had your life, I would probably kill myself."

Call Participant: Can you give another example, please?

Gary: You say, "If I had to deal with what you have to deal with, I think I'd go insane. How do you do it? How do you manage? This has got to be so hard on you." Or you can say, "Oh, ohhhh oooohhhh! Oh, my goodness! Ooooh!"

If you don't validate people's reality as they have it, they can't change it. You neither align and agree nor resist and react to it. You just allow it to be what it is and say, "Wow." If you resist and react to it because you don't want to validate their reality, what you are doing is mean. It gets them stuck in their reality even more. It doesn't allow them to come to the place where they can change it.

Call Participant: Thank you.

Call Participant: Over the last month, I've been going through my father's financial papers and mine. I don't know whether I've been grieving or whether I've been having regret about not getting to know my dad. When I was going through my papers and old Day-Timers, I went through a place where I validated myself and the space I was functioning from. And then I started grieving because until now, I didn't have an awareness of how I've been functioning my whole life. I don't know whether this is grief or regret.

Gary: Its just insanity.

Call Participant: (Laughing) I do that well.

Gary: When you say, "I've been functioning like this my whole life," is that a question? Is that a question? Or is it a conclusion?

Call Participant: I think it's was an awareness of the way I've changed and where I am now as opposed to where I was.

Gary: Okay, so you've got to acknowledge: "Wow, that was an interesting place to live." And then you ask: "What am I choosing today?" Ask that so that you go into the question.

If you go into grief, you're mourning the life you lost, which you somehow thought had some value to you. You want to *acknowledge* that life, not *validate* it. To validate it means you have to make it right somehow. Look at it all and ask: "Was that fun? What parts of it were fun?" Acknowledge what was fun, acknowledge what was good—and then move on.

Today I was talking with Dain about my wedding in the 1980s. I told him what I had worn to the rehearsal dinner. Dain said, "Wow, you remember that in such detail! Is that because it was such a hideous experience?"

I said, "No, it was fun."

The reality is there were a lot of fun times in my marriage. There were a lot of things I enjoyed and loved about it. Could I live with the woman? No. But I don't hate her and see her as a problem, nor do I see what we had as something terrible. I see it as something that was. It had its great points and it had its awful points. Nothing is ever just black and white.

That's another thing about distractor implants: All of them are designed to put us into the rightness or wrongness of everything, into the black-and-white of it all.

Dain: The rightness of the wrongness of us, and everything we are choosing, and everything we are doing.

Call Participant: What would be the type of question I could go into when I am in that space?

Gary: Well, you just acknowledged it. You just said it, "I was in that space." Were you in the space of present? Or were you in the space of past?

Call Participant: I was definitely in the past.

Gary: If you look to the past for the validation of your life, you are going to create that same past as your future. That's not going to work! That's where you have to get clear and change things.

Dain: Ask:
> What physical actualization of the reality that has never existed with regard to this situation, or with regard to my dad, or with regard to my family, (or anything else you wish to put in here) am

I now capable of generating, creating, and instituting? Everything that doesn't allow that to show up times a godzillion, will you destroy and uncreate it, please? Right and Wrong, Good and Bad, POD and POC, All 9, Shorts, Boys and Beyonds.

This will start to give you options. In addition, please listen to this call over and over and over.

Call Participant: After the last call, I had some sticky energy with anger. I thought I heard you say anger is attached to joy.

Gary: No, I said the anger covers up joy. I said that beneath the anger is the joy you could have that you wouldn't allow to show up in your life, which is why joy is so missing in this reality. Anger is designed to hide it. You can't release joy. You want to embrace the joy and release the anger. The anger hides the joy.

Call Participant: I am having issues with my body feeling bad. I feel like it's related to this.

Gary:
How much blame, shame, regret, and guilt have you locked into your body, to make it feel like shit? Everything that is times a godzillion, will you destroy and uncreate it all? Right and Wrong, Good and Bad, POD and POC, All 9, Shorts, Boys and Beyonds.

And how much awareness is your body trying to give you about what is sickening you—and you keep making blame, shame, regret, and guilt more real than the awareness? Sweet body. Everything that is times a godzillion, will you destroy and uncreate it all? Right and Wrong, Good and Bad, POD and POC, All 9, Shorts, Boys and Beyonds.

Call Participant: Gary, how can I best contribute to a friend who is going to court tomorrow?

Gary: Go in and think "truth" before every question that is asked of all the witnesses against her.

Dain: Work your magic so the judge can actually see what is actually going on that the other side has been able to lie about until now.

Call Participant: Gary and Dain, I just want to say a big thank you.

Gary: Thanks, everybody, for being on here. I hope you learned some things, and I hope they will help you dynamically.

Chapter Three
Addictive, Compulsive, Obsessive, and Perverted Points of View

Gary: Hello everyone. Welcome to our third call on distractor implants. Today we're going to talk about addictive, compulsive, obsessive, and perverted points of view.

Addictive is the idea that you can't change it. *Compulsive* is the necessity to do it. *Obsessive* is where you must think about it and figure it out so you know how to do it. It's where you have to figure it out, so it's right so you can try not to do what is wrong that you are obsessing about. Then there are *perverted points of view*. In this reality, the primary perversion is being a humanoid and not seeing the world the same way other people see it. That is the ultimate and perverse point of view.

> The ultimate in perverted point of view is seeing life with a sense of joy, not a sense of judgment. Everything you are unwilling to perceive, know, be, and receive about all that, will you destroy and uncreate it all? Right and Wrong, Good and Bad, POD and POC, All 9, Shorts, Boys and Beyonds.

Necessity

The most important part of all of this is that you have a thing called necessity. And any time there is a necessity to do, or to be, or to accomplish anything, you go into the distractor implant of addictive, compulsive, and obsessive realities.

Dain: When you define something as a necessity, you believe you don't have the choice to not do it—because it's a necessity. Or if it is a necessity to not do it, then you don't have the choice to do it. You're not recognizing that you're at choice. You go into addictive, obsessive, and compulsive points of view, which also bring up resentment, anger, rage, fury, and hate. This thing you have decided is a necessity, that you believe you wouldn't choose—that you have to choose because it is such a necessity—activates these distractor implants.

Gary:

> How many necessities do you have creating what you would call the addiction of your life? Everything that is times a godzillion, will you destroy and uncreate them all? Right and Wrong, Good and Bad, POD and POC, All 9, Shorts, Boys and Beyonds.
>
> And how many necessities do you have that create the compulsive parts of your life? Will you destroy and uncreate all those? Right and Wrong, Good and Bad, POD and POC, All 9, Shorts, Boys and Beyonds.
>
> How many necessities do you have to make you obsessive? The ultimate necessity is about being obsessive. I must to do this, I have no choice to do it; I have to do it! Everything that is times a godzillion, will you destroy and uncreate it all? Right and Wrong, Good and Bad, POD and POC, All 9, Shorts, Boys and Beyonds.

Call Participant: I've been running a lot of the body processes since the last call, and my body is requiring less sleep. But I am fighting with fixed points of view that I need to have more sleep. Can you talk about when something is a necessity in some way then it shifts from what it used to be to something else?

Gary: It's our point of view that creates a necessity. Nothing is actually a necessity. Everything is a choice. But we function, as often as possible, as if there is no choice.

We have learned to do this over time. For instance, people tell you that it is a necessity to eat three square meals a day. Well, what is a square meal? Does that mean a piece of shredded wheat? Is that an apple that has been trimmed improperly? What is a square meal? Please! It is just frigging crazy the way that we do that.

Dain: It's like a Big Mac—it comes in a square box!

Gary: You've got to have a square meal! These are all the places we buy into necessity by buying somebody else's points of view rather than actually being aware. Right now, your addictive and compulsive and obsessive points of view are primarily about the wrongness of you. They're all the ways you talk yourself into being wrong, all the ways you see you must be wrong.

> How many necessities for being wrong do you use to create this constant addictive, compulsive, and obsessive point of view about the wrongness of you? Everything that is will you destroy and uncreate it all? Right and Wrong, Good and Bad, POD and POC, All 9, Shorts, Boys and Beyonds.

Call Participant: You fried my brain with the word addictive. I have the point of view that addictive means needy or needing. What did you say addictive was?

Gary: Addictive is where you think you have no choice but to do something. Someone who drinks alcohol to an addictive state thinks that they have no real choice. They believe there is only one choice they can make—and that is to drink. They can't see any other possibility.

Many people are addicted to judgment and those people think it is a necessity to have judgment; their judgment proves who they are. These are all the ways you look at this world from the addiction to the wrongness, the judgment, the badness, and everything else.

The Ultimate Perversion Is Awareness

When you actually look at it, you see that the ultimate perversion is awareness. You realize that all the distractor implants are preparing to keep you away from awareness. The ultimate in perversion of this reality is to function from total consciousness. This reality, in and of itself, is what we've decided is *supposed* to be; it's not what actually is.

When you do addictive, compulsive, and obsessive points of view, you defend part of this reality. Wherever you think you have no choice, those are the places you are defending this reality as it is.

> How many of your own personal addictive, compulsive, and obsessive points of view are based on your need to defend or save this reality? Everything that is times a godzillion, will you destroy and uncreate it all? Right and Wrong, Good and Bad, POD and POC, All 9, Shorts, Boys and Beyonds.

Call Participant: That is exactly where I went! I went to defending or fixing the addiction. Isn't that crazy?

Gary: No, it's just the way it is here. It's the way you're supposed to do things here. It's supposed to be about defending this reality. Each one of the distractor implants are designed to take you away from total awareness, total being and get you to a place where you will eliminate everything except what this reality has fed you as true, right, and real.

So let's try this:

> What physical actualization of the addictive, compulsive, and obsessive disease of defending and saving this reality are you not acknowledging as the elimination and eradication of the perversion of total consciousness? Everything that is times a godzillion, will you destroy and uncreate it all? Right and Wrong, Good and Bad, POD and POC, All 9, Shorts, Boys and Beyonds.

Call Participant: Gary, can you explain what the perversion of total consciousness is? What does that look like?

Gary: Total consciousness is the perversion of this reality. In this reality, you are not supposed to have awareness, so total awareness is the ultimate perversion. It's what you're not ever supposed to choose.

Dain: It's the difference you are not supposed to be, which is another aspect of what is perverted here. The difference you are not supposed to be is the supposed wrongness, which, if you were willing to be it, would create the rightness of you in your own point of view. The non-judgment of the wrongness of you for the awareness you actually have.

Call Participant: You just fried my brain with that one.

Gary: What it boils down to is that in this reality, you are supposed to receive everything from the point of view that it is either right or

Addictive, Compulsive, Obsessive, & Perverted Points of View   71

wrong, good or bad, or black or white. You are not supposed to have awareness of it. You are supposed to come to conclusion and judgment and decision and computation. That is the way you are supposed live. You are supposed to live from the judgment of it all.

It is really important that you start to get how this is working rather than trying to live from the point of view that it needs to be something else. So let's run it again:

> What physical actualization of the addictive, compulsive, and obsessive disease of defending and saving this reality are you not acknowledging as the elimination and eradication of the perversion of total consciousness? Everything that is times a godzillion, will you destroy and uncreate it all please? Right and Wrong, Good and Bad, POD and POC, All 9, Shorts, Boys and Beyonds.

Call Participant: You have already talked about the food thing, but it's a really annoying factor in my life.

Gary: Are you doing food as a necessity? Is there a necessity to eat for your body? When there is a necessity for something, you end up with a whole lot of anger, and you stuff your body with the anger.

> How much of your eating as a necessity is that anger? Everything that is times a godzillion, will you destroy and uncreate it all? Right and Wrong, Good and Bad, Pod and Poc, All Nine, Shorts, Boys and Beyonds.

A lot of people go into the necessity of something and then they get angry about it. And when they do that, they often create disease in their bodies. Others create slowness in their heads. Some create an inability to function in one area or another. Some buy that everything is good as long as x, y, z occurs, and none of it has to do with awareness. Let's run it again, Dain.

Dain:

> What physical actualization of the addictive, compulsive, and obsessive disease of defending and saving this reality are you not acknowledging as the elimination and eradication of the perversion of total consciousness? Everything that is times a godzillion,

will you destroy and uncreate it, please? Right and Wrong, Good and Bad, POD and POC, All 9, Shorts, Boys and Beyonds.

How many of you know you're addicted to defending and saving this reality?

Gary: How much of this eating is defending and saving this reality? Does your body really need to eat? Or is that defending this reality too? Everyone tells you that you are supposed to eat. "You've got to eat! You are going to die if you don't eat!" It's all that kind of stuff. Have you ever asked your body what it really wants to eat? Ninety percent of the time, the body doesn't really desire to eat; it just eats because you force it to.

Dain:

> And how much of the eating is to feed the anger you have already locked into your body to maintain a particular energy or a particular vibration that you've become addicted to? Everything that is times a godzillion, will you destroy and uncreate please? Right and Wrong, Good and Bad, POD and POC, All 9, Shorts, Boys and Beyonds.

Gary: Okay, let's do it again.

> What physical actualization of the addictive, compulsive, and obsessive disease of defending and saving this reality are you not acknowledging as the elimination and eradication of the perversion of total consciousness? Everything that is times a godzillion, will you destroy and uncreate it, please? Right and Wrong, Good and Bad, POD and POC, All 9, Shorts, Boys and Beyonds.

Call Participant: Do I consider myself a perversion?

Gary: You are a perversion if you have a vague awareness of consciousness at all.

Call Participant: Yeah. That's wrong. That's a judgment.

Gary: You're supposed to be in judgment. You're supposed to live according to the rules of this reality. The problem is that no one gives you the rules. They just tell you you're supposed to live by the rules.

Call Participant: It's like a wheel, Gary. If I have a fraction of awareness, I go into the perversion, which then goes back into the judgment, which eliminates my awareness.

Gary: Whoa, whoa, whoa, no, what are you talking about?

Call Participant: I am talking about going on the wheel of judgment.

Gary: The wheel of judgment is not the perversion. Consciousness is the perversion.

Call Participant: The minute I consider myself a perversion, I go into the judgment of it, because I consider perversion a judgment.

Gary: Perversion is not a judgment; perversion is awareness. You go into judgment in order to get other distractor implants to work for you, to keep you defending this reality and living as though there is a necessity to live according to the rules of this reality.

Call Participant: Awesome. I assumed that anything that was a perversion was a wrongness.

THE REAL PERVERSION OF THIS REALITY IS CONSCIOUSNESS

Gary: I understand that. But that is everything as it is done here. The real perversion is consciousness. It's the perversion of this reality. You're not supposed to be conscious in this reality. If you are willing to live by the rules of this reality and be subject to them, and if you are willing to defend this reality and to defend necessity as truth, you cannot function in consciousness and not go into judgment of yourself.

Call Participant: Thank you, Gary.

Call Participant: You speak of the "they," who do the implants. Who is "they" other than our parents or ancestors?

Gary: It probably happened four trillion years ago, so it doesn't matter who "they" are. What matters is that you have to align and agree with it or resist and react to it for it to occur. So to that degree, we are responsible for this ourselves. We are choosing to align and agree with it or resist and react to it, which is what allows it to occur.

Dain: It's that way with everything. Rather than asking, "What is it? Where is it coming from? Who did it to us?" you have to get to the point where you ask: "Okay, what am I choosing here?"

Gary: There is no "why?" in awareness. If you go to "why?" you are out of awareness. The moment you go to "why?" you have lost awareness, and you will never get it back. Don't go to the "why?" If you do, you will go into the wrongness of you and stop all this up.

Dain: Here's something you can do that will assist in every area of your life: Every time you start to say, "Oh this happened," stop. POC and POD it and ask: "What can I create?" In other words, rather than "This happened," go to "I created this." If you cut out "This happened" and go to "I created this," very quickly you will begin to realize "Wow, I am creating everything that is showing up! Somehow, I am contributing something to it!"

This gives you a different place to be. It's where you start to be more of the perversion consciousness is, which is the awareness that you are actually creating reality. It is not happening to you.

Call Participant: In the past week or so, I have noticed that I have been having a lot of fun. I've been enjoying my job and the other things I am doing. My massage business has taken off and I'm feeling more prosperous. I got the idea that it would be fun to start a choir. The energy on it was really cool. Later that day, I was talking with someone, and as soon as I mentioned the choir, the conversation got all twisted. The person said, "Wow, is that a perverted point of view?" as if something that would bring you great joy was perverse. It was such a twist!

Gary: Joy, happiness, and awareness are a perversion of this reality.

Dain: Abundance, ease, peace, possibility, no judgment, and not having a problem are all perversions of this reality. They come to you from awareness and consciousness. Consciousness is the way you have and be all of those things. It's the way you can choose them.

Gary: The twisting is what you have to do so you can be wrong, so that you can go into those addictive, compulsive, and obsessive, points of view. It's to make sure you continually show up as less than you. Let's run this again:

Addictive, Compulsive, Obsessive, & Perverted Points of View

> What physical actualization of the addictive, compulsive, and obsessive disease of defending and saving this reality are you not acknowledging as the elimination and eradication of the perversion of total consciousness? Everything that is times a godzillion, will you destroy and uncreate it, please? Right and Wrong, Good and Bad, POD and POC, All 9, Shorts, Boys and Beyonds.

Call Participant: I think that for me, the addictive, compulsive, and obsessive points of view are mainly with relationship, and I flip between that and perversion.

Gary: You guys take these single areas and you say things like, "In this area, this is what's so." But, it's not what's so. You do it in all aspects of your life. For example, how many times do you judge yourself a day? Is that addictive, compulsive, and obsessive? Yeah, non-stop!

So it is not just in relationships; it's simply more obvious in relationships, because the other person is trying so desperately to love you, and in order to make sure they don't, you have to obsessively, compulsively, and continuously find something wrong with them or with you. Isn't that cool? And we all know there is a necessity to have a relationship right?

> Everything that is times a godzillion, will you destroy and uncreate please? Right and Wrong, Good and Bad, POD and POC, All 9, Shorts, Boys and Beyonds.

Necessity or Choice

You need to walk around asking: "Am I doing this out of necessity or choice?" Once you get clear about whether you're doing it out of necessity or choice, you'll change all these areas dynamically.

Call Participant: When I am facilitating people, it is clear to me that there are obsessive, compulsive, and obsessive things that are never spoken of. For example, most people won't acknowledge that they obsessively pick stuff on their body or obsessively lock the house over and over again or do other kinds of typical obsessive-compulsive things.

Gary: They don't notice.

Call Participant: They don't notice. That's it exactly. What could you add to opening that awareness for them? Or can you—if they just don't want to?

Gary: If they don't want it, you can't do anything about it. You have to wait until somebody asks a question. But you also have to get that the necessity of never speaking about things, the necessity of keeping of secrets, the necessity of keeping things private, and the necessity of keeping things under cover locks them back in to the distractor disease.

> Everything that is times a godzillion, will you destroy and uncreate please? Right and Wrong, Good and Bad, POD and POC, All 9, Shorts, Boys and Beyonds.

It's not about doing the not-necessity, or the un-necessity, or the non-necessity as a dismissal. That is the dismissal of something; it is not necessarily choice. Dismissal is not a choice.

> How many not-, un-, and non- necessities do you have keeping you in your personal addictive, compulsive, and obsessive reality? Everything that is times a godzillion, will you destroy and uncreate it all? Right and Wrong, Good and Bad, POD and POC, All 9, Shorts, Boys and Beyonds.

Call Participant: Gary, it almost feels like that's the fabric that holds all the limitations in place.

Gary: Not *almost*, it *is*. It is all a factor. Notice that we all have a place where our reality ceases. It's like being the distractor implant is more real than having your own reality and actually being active.

Dain: Look around. How many people in the world are trapped in these distractor implants? And how much are they valuing or not valuing consciousness?

People think that if their eyes are open, they are conscious—and that is even more conscious than they want to be. They are not seeking more, and so much of what has been perpetrated as consciousness on the planet isn't consciousness. It's a lie that it is consciousness; it's a conclusion and an answer. It was supposedly something better than what came before it.

Addictive, Compulsive, Obsessive, & Perverted Points of View   77

If you realize that it is seen as more valuable in this reality for you to function from distractor implants and from other people's points of view, you start to recognize where some aspect of this has been predetermined for you as the necessity for the reality you must choose. It's a perversion if you choose anything other than that.

Call Participant: Can you define perversion for me, please?

Gary: Perversion is not buying this reality.

Dain:

> What physical actualization of the addictive, compulsive, and obsessive disease of defending and saving this reality are you not acknowledging as the elimination and eradication of the perversion of total consciousness? Everything that is times a godzillion, will you destroy and uncreate it, please? Right and Wrong, Good and Bad, POD and POC, All 9, Shorts, Boys and Beyonds.

Call Participant: This is fascinating. That means it is a necessity to have a family and to have children, and they call it joy. Wow!

Gary: Having kids is some fun times, and a lot of not-fun times. It is not all awesome and luck and wonder, and it's not all fabulous and great. Rather than being a necessity, if you are aware, you would have an awareness of what you are going to get with a family and children, and it would give you a place where you can chose.

Once again, the ultimate perversion is total awareness. This is what real perversion is—total awareness. You have been given the lie that perversion is anything that is bad. And the most bad thing on planet Earth is awareness. It is the one thing everyone tries to avoid. Can we run this again?

Dain:

> What physical actualization of the addictive, compulsive, and obsessive disease of defending and saving this reality are you not acknowledging as the elimination and eradication of the perversion of total consciousness? Everything that is times a godzillion, will you destroy and uncreate it, please? Right and Wrong, Good and Bad, Pod and Poc, All Nine, Shorts, Boys and Beyonds.

Call Participant: The word resistance keeps coming up when we talk about perversion. Are we in resistance somewhere when we try to undo this reality?

Gary: No, you're in defense. If you fight it, or fix it, or choose it, you are defending it or trying to save it. If you are trying to go against it, you're fighting hard to save it, because you only fight what you really would like to have.

Call Participant: So if you're trying to create change in it, you're still in resistance to it?

Gary: Yes. And you're doing that rather than having the total awareness of what would be different that could be more and greater than what we currently have. You've got to be willing to employ this reality to take care of you and to service you instead of becoming an employee of this reality and working really hard to make this reality work.

Wherever you're short of money, wherever your life isn't abundant, wherever you're trying desperately to fix a relationship, or wherever you're trying to undo something that has been there since you were born—or eight years old or whatever—all of these things are about the idea that you have to somehow fix or defend the reality you currently have, not that you can choose a different one, one that comes from the ability to recognize that you are actually aware.

Call Participant: So you don't want to talk about this from the standpoint that it's is a different way to change your world. You want to talk about it from the standpoint that this is a different awareness you can have.

Gary: This is an awareness you can have, and if you have this awareness, what kind of reality can you create and generate that hasn't existed yet?

Call Participant: I am guilty of having shared this information with people because I want to change the world.

Gary: Well, we all have. We think we have to change the world rather than creating a world that actually works. If you looked around and saw how little there is that works on planet Earth, would you try to

Addictive, Compulsive, Obsessive, & Perverted Points of View 79

change it? Would you try to fix it? Or would you be willing to create something that has never existed?

Call Participant: I think that the problem for me is not that I always believed that this reality is real, or that I have to do everything that everyone else is doing, or that I had to have their point of view. The problem was—how do you create a change that everyone else is willing to live in?

Gary: You just said it again. You asked, "How do you create a change?" It's not about creating a change; it's about creating a difference.

Call Participant: Do you do that by staying within yourself and staying in what you believe in?

Gary: You cannot do that. Consciousness includes everything and everyone and judges nothing. If you are trying to change things and you're trying to stay within yourself, you are trying to withdraw from this reality, which is defending the rightness of the fact that it is wrong and you're wrong.

Call Participant: I have to think about that one.

Gary: It is different than you think. You have been trying forever to change this reality. Have you succeeded?

Call Participant: No.

Gary: No. Trying to change it is based on the idea that it is good. Years ago when I was in the upholstery business, people would come to me and say, "I want you to fix this couch." The couch would have really straight arms. People would say, "I want you to make fluffy arms."

I would say, "You can't make fluffy arms out of a straight-arm couch."

They'd say, "Yeah, but I want a different couch!"

I'd say, "Your couch isn't made to have fluffy arms, so you can't get fluffy arms."

"Yeah, but I want fluffy arms!"

"Well, then go buy a different couch."

"But I want to reupholster this one."

"But you can't reupholster it and make it look or feel like what you're asking for."

"Well, then I am going to buy a new couch."

"Yeah, that is what I told you to do."

You're trying to reupholster a world that doesn't work.

> Everything that is times a godzillion, will you destroy and uncreate it all? Right and Wrong, Good and Bad, POD and POC, All 9, Shorts, Boys and Beyonds.

If you make it a necessity to change the world, do you have choice? Or do you always have to judge whether you're changing it or not? You have to judge. You cannot have true choice as long as there is any necessity to change it, or to make it better, or to be able to survive it, or any of those things that are all necessities that don't give you choice.

What you want is that perverted place in which you have total choice and total awareness. But you assume that *perversion* is wrong, that it's a badness. The definition of perversion is that which does not fit in other people's normal reality.

> Everything that is times a godzillion, will you destroy and uncreate it all? Right and Wrong, Good and Bad, POD and POC, All 9, Shorts, Boys and Beyonds.

Call Participant: So perversion is ease, joy, and glory?

Gary: Yes.

Call Participant: I have achieved perversion quite well in some places, but I assumed that I was not achieving or doing the right thing, and that I should try harder.

Gary: What made you decide that you were wrong?

Addictive, Compulsive, Obsessive, & Perverted Points of View   81

Call Participant: Other people don't live like I do. They don't think like I do. I never wanted to have children; I never wanted to get married. I never wanted to have any of those things. I wasn't in resistance to anything; they were simply choices. I just didn't want those things.

Gary: Okay.

Call Participant: But that doesn't lessen the judgments that come at me about them, and I find myself wanting and longing about them…

Gary: As long as you think somebody has judgment of you or your choices, you are at a loss and you have lost. That is what the addictive, compulsive and obsessive part of this thing is about. It's where you always start to see you as a judge-able offense.

You have to be willing to have a different reality in which you respond to the judgment with "Okay, thanks for judging me" or "Oh my gosh, you're judging me, but thanks for judging me."

> Everything that is times a godzillion, will you destroy and uncreate it all? Right and Wrong, Good and Bad, POD and POC, All 9, Shorts, Boys and Beyonds.

If you can be in that place that is truly perverted…

Call Participant: (Laughing) Sorry, I have to laugh.

Dain: Good.

Gary: It's an evil little laugh!

Call Participant: It's great!

Gary: Notice how much happier that makes you feel?

Call Participant: It's a relief not to have to try to fix myself.

Gary: When you are always in a state of trying to fix something, you're always trying to defend this reality. Whether it's you, this reality, or anything else, you've got to come to a place where you recognize, "Oh, I have a different choice than most people have! I choose differently than they do!" It's not "I am right" or "I am wrong." It's "I am just different." Being different is perverted in this reality. Anything that isn't in standard operating procedure is perverted.

Call Participant: Is trying to make perversion into a success as much resistance as trying to fix it? Is there some use for that perversion?

Gary: You haven't used perversion to create success because you haven't asked, "Is this a necessity for me? Or is this a choice? Am I doing what I am doing from choice?" As long as you have any necessity about anything, you are not choosing. You are being run by something outside of you.

Dain: If you are saying that it is a necessity to prove you are being successful from this other point of view, or that it is a necessity to prove you have it right, you're not functioning from the ease of the choice of it.

But if it is just a choice and an awareness, "I've got different stuff going on than anybody else does," then you have the freedom to allow your choice to contribute to your life and you are not limited by it.

Call Participant: It feels more like that last one, but I will definitely review this carefully.

Dain: Put an "Under Careful Review and Construction" sign on your bedroom door.

Call Participant: (Laughing) That is nice.

Dain:

> What physical actualization of the addictive, compulsive, and obsessive disease of defending and saving this reality are you not acknowledging as the elimination and eradication of the perversion of total consciousness? Everything that is times a godzillion, will you destroy and uncreate it, please? Right and Wrong, Good and Bad, POD and POC, All 9, Shorts, Boys and Beyonds.

Remember when we talked about anger, rage, fury and hate, and we said that anger and potency are closely related? A little shift or a twist occurs when you align and agree with something. There is base energy that's true for you as a being. You then align and agree with that, and it gets twisted.

The energy of the difference that you *are* is different from this reality. When you align and agree or resist and react, it allows the distractor implant to be implanted and explanted.[7] Without that alignment and agreement or that resistance and reaction, the implant wouldn't exist. Without the necessity of making any of that right or wrong, none of this could exist in the same way.

Gary:

> What physical actualization of the addictive, compulsive, and obsessive disease of defending and saving this reality are you not acknowledging as the elimination and eradication of the perversion of total consciousness? Everything that is times a godzillion, will you destroy and uncreate it, please? Right and Wrong, Good and Bad, POD and POC, All 9, Shorts, Boys and Beyonds.

Call Participant: Dain, did you just say that when I align and agree, I open doors for distractor implants to jump in? Is that correct?

Gary: Yes, that is correct. It doesn't matter whether you align or agree or you resist and react. Either one of them takes you out of choice into necessity. Have you ever noticed that when you have an awareness about anything and you try to share it with somebody, they say, "Oh, you're wrong," or "Oh, you're crazy!"? They can't see what you see.

Dain: It also occurs when someone asks you to tell them when they are doing a behavior they say they don't want to do. If you say, "Remember when you asked me to tell you when you are acting like that person you don't want to act like? Well, you're doing it." If they are not ready to hear it, they'll get angry.

Gary: And they are never ready to hear it, so don't ever believe it when people say, "Tell me when I am doing that when I shouldn't be doing it." Don't bother, because they are lying.

---

[7] Implants are things that have been done to the body in one lifetime or another. Explants are things that have been done outside the body, in the etheric bodies around the physical body. They have an action on the body, but they're not in it.

Dain: If you say they're lying, they are never going to believe it. But the fact is, they are lying. They never want to know that stuff; they just say they do.

Gary: So let's run that again, Dr. Dain.

Dain:

> What physical actualization of the addictive, compulsive, and obsessive disease of defending and saving this reality are you not acknowledging as the elimination and eradication of the perversion of total consciousness? Everything that is times a godzillion, will you destroy and uncreate it, please? Right and Wrong, Good and Bad, POD and POC, All 9, Shorts, Boys and Beyonds.

Gary: It looks like we are actually getting somewhere. Can that be true?

Dain: Yeah, it can.

Gary: Cool.

> So what necessity are you using to create the illness in your body? Everything that is times a godzillion, will you destroy and uncreate it all? Right and Wrong, Good and Bad, POD and POC, All 9, Shorts, Boys and Beyonds.

> What necessity are you using and what defense of this reality are you choosing to create the problems you're having in your marriage? Everything that is times a godzillion, will you destroy and uncreate please? Right and Wrong, Good and Bad, POD and POC, All 9, Shorts, Boys and Beyonds.

> What physical actualizations of the terminal and incumbent disease of necessity are you not acknowledging as the superior source for the creation of the no-choice universe you believe creates your reality? Everything that is times a godzillion, will you destroy and uncreate it, please? Right and Wrong, Good and Bad, POD and POC, All 9, Shorts, Boys and Beyonds.

Addictive, Compulsive, Obsessive, & Perverted Points of View   85

Dain:
> What physical actualizations of the terminal and incumbent disease of necessity are you not acknowledging as the superior source for the creation of the no-choice universe you believe creates your reality? Everything that is times a godzillion, will you destroy and uncreate it, please? Right and Wrong, Good and Bad, POD and POC, All 9, Shorts, Boys and Beyonds.

Call Participant: I now get why you put the word addictive in. Somehow I knew that perversion is total awareness and now it is so much clearer. I just wanted to say thank you. It is so mind-changing to hear that perversion is total awareness and total consciousness! Thank you very much, both of you!

Gary: You're welcome.

> What physical actualization of the terminal and incumbent disease of necessity are you not acknowledging as the superior source for the creation of the no-choice universe you believe creates your reality? Everything that is times a godzillion, will you destroy and uncreate it, please? Right and Wrong, Good and Bad, POD and POC, All 9, Shorts, Boys and Beyonds.

The Ultimate Source

Notice that I said, "the superior source," because the ultimate source should be you. You think there is a source that is superior to you that has caused you to have a no-choice reality. There is no such thing! You are in charge, folks!

> Everything that is times a godzillion, will you destroy and uncreate it all? Right and Wrong, Good and Bad, POD and POC, All 9, Shorts, Boys and Beyonds.

> What physical actualization of the terminal and incumbent disease of necessity are you not acknowledging as the superior source for the creation of the no-choice universe you believe creates your reality? Everything that is times a godzillion, will you destroy and uncreate it, please? Right and Wrong, Good and Bad, POD and POC, All 9, Shorts, Boys and Beyonds.

Call Participant: What came up for me is that the no-choice universe is my reality.

Gary: Yes, because you think there is something out there beyond you. You think there's something that is above you, that is greater than you. That puts you in a place where you have no choice. For you, no choice is more real than choice.

And if you have the no-choice point of view, it means that wherever you decided you have no choice, you eliminate the capacity to change anything you would like to change. Change ceases the moment you have the no-choice universe.

Call Participant: Thank you.

Gary: You have the capacity change anything you will.

> What physical actualization of the terminal and incumbent disease of necessity are you not acknowledging as the superior source for the creation of the no-choice universe you believe creates your reality? Everything that is times a godzillion, will you destroy and uncreate it, please? Right and Wrong, Good and Bad, Pod and Poc, All Nine, Shorts, Boys and Beyonds.

Gary: I am going to change the wording on this slightly:

> What physical actualization of the terminal and incumbent disease of necessity are you not acknowledging as the superior source for the creation of the no-choice universe you believe creates and dominates your reality? Everything that is times a godzillion, will you destroy and uncreate it, please? Right and Wrong, Good and Bad, Pod and Poc, All Nine, Shorts, Boys and Beyonds.

Oh, that's good! That made it worse.

Participants: (Laughing)

Gary:

> What physical actualization of the terminal and incumbent disease of necessity are you not acknowledging as the superior source for the creation of the no-choice universe you believe creates and dominates your reality? Everything that is times a godzillion, will

you destroy and uncreate it, please? Right and Wrong, Good and Bad, POD and POC, All 9, Shorts, Boys and Beyonds.

Call Participant: Wow, "superior source" just moved me into all the greater mysteries.

Gary: Yeah, because would you, as an infinite being, if you had true awareness, would you have any mysteries?

Call Participant: Apparently not.

Gary: No, we do a whole lot of stuff to create the idea that there is a superior source who has control of us. It's the way we create destiny and karma and all those things.

Call Participant: It's also how we run our bodies. That seems to be a mystery to many of us—how we run our bodies, what we do with them, what they can do, how they can heal.

Gary: Yes, it's a perversion to actually understand your body.

Call Participant: That you can, or that you can't?

Gary: If you can, it's a perversion. So you try not to, so you can have the mystery, so you can believe that there is a higher source that can control you. How fun is that?

Dain: Because if you can't even control the fundamental thing called your body and get it to grow three arms and four legs and all the things you should be able to do, you believe that you have the least potency and the least capacity to create change and choose. It's your constant enforcement of a no-choice universe.

Gary: And you have the addictive, compulsive, and obsessive points of view that you somehow have no known control over your body, you are not the creator of it, and you actually don't have the ability to change it.

Call Participant: Ah! That is like punching me!

Gary: Sorry!

Call Participant: Thank you.

Gary: That is not my point of view. We have been doing all the body classes to give people more awareness of their body. The Advanced Body Class has some new stuff that is beginning to have dynamic effects. If it continues to go the way it has been going, it's going to be just wondrous. So keep your fingers crossed that we finally have the edge on this area of insanity, and that we are going to create a change here too.

> Everything that is times a godzillion, will you destroy and uncreate it all? Right and Wrong, Good and Bad, POD and POC, All 9, Shorts, Boys and Beyonds.

Dain:

> What physical actualization of the terminal and incumbent disease of necessity are you not acknowledging as the superior source for the creation of the no-choice universe you believe creates and dominates your reality? Everything that is times a godzillion, will you destroy and uncreate it, please? Right and Wrong, Good and Bad, POD and POC, All 9, Shorts, Boys and Beyonds.

Call Participant: That would be everything that is. We are the physical actualization of all of that.

Gary: Yes, and more—and we have not been being that. We have been functioning from the rules of this reality. We have been defending this reality and being the saviors of this reality by trying to fix what doesn't work instead of creating what will work.

Call Participant: I just love that. This is just such a relief! You can't imagine.

Gary: Ah, I can! It was a relief for me to realize that.

Call Participant: I was just looking at the necessity of privacy, and I was aware that in order to choose to have things be private, I am trying to avoid judgment. Am I therefore thinking that judgment is more powerful and a greater source than me?

Gary: Yes, isn't that cool?

Call Participant: It's really brewing.

Gary: Yes, it's judgment as a higher source.

Dain: My question is: "How well is it working?"

Call Participant: It's not.

Gary: That is the funny part about it—we do all this stuff and it doesn't work, and we keep doing it as though somehow it's going to work. Are we the stupidest creatures on the planet or what?

Call Participant: Can we POD and POC some more judgments?

Gary:
> Everything that is times a godzillion, will you destroy and uncreate it all? Right and Wrong, Good and Bad, POD and POC, All 9, Shorts, Boys and Beyonds.

Call Participant: Thank you.

Gary: Let's do it again, Dr. Dain!

Dain:
> What physical actualization of the terminal and incumbent disease of necessity are you not acknowledging as the superior source for the creation of the no-choice universe you believe creates and dominates your reality? Everything that is times a godzillion, will you destroy and uncreate it, please? Right and Wrong, Good and Bad, POD and POC, All 9, Shorts, Boys and Beyonds.

Gary: There are important aspects here:

1. Addictive, compulsive, and obsessive only occur when you put anything into necessity. You have to create a necessity for something in order for it to become addictive, compulsive, or obsessive.
2. Or you have make it not-necessary, un-necessary, or non-necessary to have addictive, compulsive, and obsessive things going on.
3. The real perversion in life is happiness, oneness, and consciousness. That is the perversion in this reality. Nothing else is as perverted as actual and total awareness.

If you really want to get over this stuff, you've got to choose total awareness. You can get over all the distractor implants from total awareness. But as long as you are not doing total awareness, these distractor implants can control you completely and utterly. Please get that if it is a necessity and not a choice, it's not awareness.

Dain: You can get a lot of freedom, if in addition to listening to these clearing statements over and over again in the next couple of weeks, every time you notice yourself being wrong, being resistant to something, or resenting something, you ask: "How many necessities do I have creating this?" And then destroy and uncreate them. POC and POD them.

As you come out of necessity, you will also come out of the ability to be limited, destroyed, and held down by distractor implants. They won't be able to have the same effect on you as before because you will be functioning from choice.

Gary: A lady who was doing this stuff about necessity discovered that she would go into anger instantaneously because she had this necessity to feel powerful. When she got over the necessity to get angry and started looking at "What is my choice here?" the anger would dissipate instantaneously.

She had been trying to function from a place where she had a sense of power, and it became a place where she had the power and potency of her. Instead of reacting to anything, (which is what distractor implants are designed to get us to do—to get you to react not to act) she started taking action. This created huge changes for her, with herself and her body, with everybody she talked to, and with everybody she interacted with.

So it's a not big thing. It's just everything.

Necessity or Choice?

You will create a totally different reality if you start to function from asking: "Is this a necessity or choice?" Simply do everything you do from the space of asking if it's a necessity or a choice. Is it a necessity for you to eat eggs and bacon for breakfast? Or is it a choice? Is it a necessity for you to drink coffee before you're awake? Or is it a choice?

Dain: Is it a necessity to eat raw food in order for you to think you are being healthy? Or is it a choice?

Gary: Is it necessity to eat properly in order to create your body? Or is it a choice?

Dain: I was at breakfast this morning with a guy who works with us, setting up interviews and things while I am in Australia. He looked at what was on the breakfast table and he said, "You have an interview coming up with a men's health magazine, and what you have here is exactly what they need to see."

I asked, "What are you talking about?"

He said, "The way you're eating, what you have on the table that you are going consume—it is not the way it is supposed to be done at all."

I said, "What? You mean my Cocoa Puffs with granola in it? My eggs with ketchup? My bacon? The cheese with meat on it? The bread with jam? What do you mean? This is not the way to create a healthy body?"

All the things we decided are necessities keep us from having different choices.

Gary: And there are a whole lot of things we buy from others as a necessity, like it's a necessity to put your clothes on. Well it's not a necessity, but it might be a choice. If it's cold outside, it might be a nice choice to wear something warmer—but you've got to ask whether you are doing it from necessity or choice.

Why are you doing what you're doing—in every aspect of your life?

Is it necessity to not have enough money? Or is it a choice to not have enough money? Ask: "Am I doing this from necessity or choice here? What is the necessity I am functioning from that is keeping me from having all the money I would like to have? Is it a choice to have no money? Wow, I had no idea."

You've got to be willing to have the awareness of the necessity or the choice. Please work with this in the next couple of weeks, because it is going to create some magnificent changes for you, if you're willing to have them.

Are there any questions?

Call Participant: We have barely talked about addiction, which is interesting, since it is such a big issue. What makes addiction such a big issue?

Gary: What you have decided. Addiction is not a big issue. Addiction is the reaction you have to everything, as though that is more important than your awareness. Addiction is the way in which you eliminate awareness.

> Every addiction that you have created to create an elimination of your awareness, will you destroy and uncreate it all that? Right and Wrong, Good and Bad, POD and POC, All 9, Shorts, Boys and Beyonds.

Call Participant: I want to ask about sleep again. Rather than saying, "I have to get this amount of sleep to create the body so I don't feel tired," should I ask the body, "Body, do you require sleep? If so, how much?"

Gary: No, I wouldn't ask that question. I would ask: "Is it a necessity to sleep this long—or is it a choice?" It is very simple.

Dain and I have discovered in the last week that we've been waking up at a time in the morning when there are not a lot of people around that we can interact with, and that is the time we are most generative and creative. We tend to think being generative and creative is about getting up and doing something rather than using that generative and creative energy to create a change in the aspect of our lives, our business, our reality, or our bodies, that we haven't asked for.

In the instant when you wake up ask:

- Am I through sleeping?
- What is going on here?
- Is this my generative and creative time?

- What generative and creative energies do I have available now and how can I use them to expand my life?"

That is what we have been doing. We wake up, we get up, and we use the generative and creative energies we have available to expand the different areas of our life and to change the areas of our life that are not working exactly as we would like them to.

Call Participant: Thank you, Gary.

Gary: You are welcome.

Call Participant: Is there a difference between necessary and necessity?

Gary: Not really.

Call Participant: Okay, so both do the same thing?

Gary: Is it necessary for me to pick up my kids from school? If it was my choice, I would leave the little shits there...

Participants: (Laughing)

Gary: We make it a necessity to pick them up because we don't want to be seen as bad parents.

Call Participant: Is there something between necessity and choice? If you are not in necessity or choice, where are you?

Gary: You are in some kind of la-la land that doesn't really exist. It's either necessity or choice; those are the two places we function from at this point in time. There is nothing between awareness and not awareness, which is what necessity creates.

Call Participant: I have another question about sleep. If I don't get as much sleep as I'm used to for multiple nights in a row and I'm feeling a little bit tired or I'm a little bit off in the body, is having this tiredness a necessity—or am I choosing it?

Gary: Probably for you, there is a necessity of sleeping a certain number of hours, or the necessity of feeling a certain way when you wake up. When I wake up and feel tired, I ask, "Body, are you really tired?"

It says, "No."

I ask, "So is this somebody else's?"

"Yes."

"Okay, fine!" and I am over it.

Ninety-nine percent of the time, you don't ask, "Is this mine?" You assume "I am tired!" And okay, you may be tired—but *you* don't sleep—ever. Only your *body* sleeps. So ask: "Body are you tired?" and it usually says, "No."

The necessity of long hours of sleep has been impelled at us. You are told as a kid that you have to go to sleep or you will be tired at school tomorrow. It's all that kind of stuff. When you're a little kid, you never get tired…until you get tired, and then you lie down, fall asleep, and you're gone. You just crash. Kids don't lie down and try to go to sleep like adults.

This applies to other things as well. Dain noticed that the idea of changing his hormonal balances was being impelled at him as something he was supposed to do at his age—but it wasn't true for him. That might apply to one or two of you as well.

> Everything that is times a godzillion, will you destroy and uncreate all of those necessities please? Right and Wrong, Good and Bad, POD and POC, All 9, Shorts, Boys and Beyonds.

Call Participant: Thank you!

Gary: You're welcome. Okay, folks, we are at the end of our time. Please think about this, look at it, and listen to this call again, because it will give you a lot more clarity. Thanks to all of you for being here tonight.

Dain: Thanks to you addicted, compulsive, obsessive, perverted, wonderful people.

Chapter Four
Love, Sex, Jealousy, and Peace

Gary: Hello everyone. Today our subject is the distractor implants love, sex, jealousy, and peace. The reality is that none of these actually exist on planet Earth.

Love

Love has about eight trillion definitions, so when you say, "I love you" to somebody, they actually have no idea what you are talking about. They *think* they have an idea of what you're talking about, because from their point of view *love* means x, y, z. It doesn't have anything to do with what your point of view or definition of love is.

Dain: With love, it's not just the definitions that you look up in the dictionary; there are also all kinds of activations, so when you hear it from different people in different contexts, it means different things to you.

When you say, "I love you" to somebody, you'll notice a contraction in their world—or a contraction in yours—right after you say it. There's an energetic activation that this particular word tends to bring up, which is always the creation of more limitation, not more possibilities.

Gary: If you say, "I love you" to your kids, is it the same as when you say, "I love you" to your lover? Is it the same thing or a different thing? What are you actually talking about when you say, "I love you?" What are you actually functioning from? What are you actually creating from? This is the distractor element of this implant. It's about creating confusion; it's never about creating clarity.

> Everything you have done to create love as the distractor implant of the entire universe, which keeps you from actually having any awareness, will you destroy and uncreate all of that? Right and Wrong, Good and Bad, POD and POC, All 9, Shorts, Boys and Beyonds.

Dain: We tend to create love as so valuable that we would rather have the love and the confusion that goes with it than the clarity and the space that comes with awareness.

Gary: That is the whole idea with these distractor implants. They are designed to create a place where you have no clue what you're actually asking for. You only know you're asking for something that should not be delivered.

> All the things you have asked for that cannot be delivered, will you destroy and uncreate all that, please? Right and Wrong, Good and Bad, POD and POC, All 9, Shorts, Boys and Beyonds.

Jealousy

So that is love. Jealousy goes back to Saint Jealous the Divine, which was a cult about never allowing anything to change. It was about holding onto the physical form of something so it would never change or disintegrate.

You were jealous of your furniture, so your furniture would not disintegrate, would not go away, would not cease to exist in its present form. Nothing in your life could fall apart. That was the original definition of Saint Jealous.

Dain: You could look at the things that most people get jealous about—sex and relationships, somebody flirting with somebody else, somebody having sex with somebody else—and the concept would be "My relationship is going to fall apart if this occurs. Oh, no! I can't have my relationship change because it's such a vital part of my life."

Obviously this is a totally different take on jealousy. Recognizing that jealousy is about trying to hold things in place so they don't change starts unlocking the area of jealousy for you in a totally different way.

How many of you have committed to Saint Jealous the Divine as a way of making sure nothing in your life disintegrates?

> All of you who have taken oaths, vows, swearings, fealties, comealties,[8] and commitments to Saint Jealous the Divine, will you destroy and uncreate all that times a godzillion, please? Right and Wrong, Good and Bad, POD and POC, All 9, Shorts, Boys and Beyonds.

Dain: How many of you have done the ultimate and become Saint Jealous the Divine?

Gary: Well, they don't actually become Saint Jealous the Divine; they take over the role of being Saint Jealous the Divine.

> How many of you have dedicated your lives to being Saint Jealous the Divine? Everything that is, will you destroy and uncreate it all? Right and Wrong, Good and Bad, POD and POC, All 9, Shorts, Boys and Beyonds.

SEX

Let's talk about sex. Sex is what? Sex is when you're walking tall, looking good, feeling good, and strutting your stuff. It is not about the copulation you have. Unfortunately most of us define sex as copulation.

> Wherever you define copulation as sex, you have to, of necessity, make yourself wrong for looking good, feeling good, or strutting your stuff. Everything that is times a godzillion, will you destroy and uncreate it all? Right and Wrong, Good and Bad, POD and POC, All 9, Shorts, Boys and Beyonds.

---

[8] A fealty is a promise from feudal times, such as when a serf swore his loyalty to a king in return for his protection. A comealty is a fealty that has melded into your physical structure. It's like a blood oath on steroids.

Dain: Everybody has the point of view that putting the body parts together is sex—but how much of the copulation you have had in your life felt like it created more space and more desire to look good and feel good and to strut your stuff? And how much of it created less?

Gary:

> Everywhere that you bought that less equals sex, and everywhere you denied that looking good, feeling good, strutting your stuff, and being expansive was actually truthness, will you destroy and uncreate all that? Right and Wrong, Good and Bad, POD and POC, All 9, Shorts, Boys and Beyonds.

> And everywhere you decided that if you could just copulate, you would get a lot more of that looking good, feeling good, and strutting your stuff—but it didn't work out that way—so all you got was another chance to go into judgment of you, hence the distractor implant of this thing, will you destroy and uncreate it, please? Right and Wrong, Good and Bad, POD and POC, All 9, Shorts, Boys and Beyonds.

Peace

The thing that holds all of this in existence is peace. Where do you see peace existing on planet Earth? You don't, do you? Peace doesn't exist anywhere.

Dain: Actually, it exists out in nature where there are no people.

Gary: Oh yeah, that. Other than that, peace doesn't exist.

> So everywhere in the human race, where peace is what you're seeking and peace is what you are not having, will you destroy and uncreate all that? Right and Wrong, Good and Bad, POD and POC, All 9, Shorts, Boys and Beyonds.

The thing about peace that's unique and true is the basic being of you, as a being. You have a sense of peace. And with peace comes joy and possibility. So why is peace a distractor implant? Instead of having peace with what is, you try to create a problem so you have something to overcome so you can discover the peace you think you will have if you overcome the problem.

> Everything that is times a godzillion, will you destroy and uncreate it all? Right and Wrong, Good and Bad, POD and POC, All 9, Shorts, Boys and Beyonds.

Peace is a natural state of being. And if you were truly at peace with things, would you stop your partner from copulating with somebody else? Or would you be willing to see them copulating with someone else as a contribution to their lives?

Whenever you are trying to have a sense of peace, you're trying to create a place where you feel okay about what is going on in your life. It's where you feel good about what is happening in your life and you feel like you don't have to throw any attention at it, which means you don't have to have awareness. And when you don't have awareness, do you have possibility, choice, and question, and contribution? No.

> Everything that is times a godzillion, will you destroy and uncreate it all? Right and Wrong, Good and Bad, POD and POC, All 9, Shorts, Boys and Beyonds.

Peace is the key that locks you up in all these other places, because you don't actually believe that peace exists.

I was talking with a guy the other day who said, "I am getting divorced. My life is over. It's terrible. I love this woman and I want to be with her."

I said, "Bullshit!"

He said, "What?"

I said, "Bullshit. When did you leave this relationship? More than five years ago or less?"

He said, "Oh my God, more than five years ago."

I said, "Yeah, so six years ago you left the relationship and now you're pissed at her for getting a boyfriend? What are you talking about, dude? This is frigging nuts."

That is pretty much the way people function. They try to prove they are right and the other person is wrong, which is not peace. Real peace is "If I'm not the best you ever had, go find someone else." That is my point of view.

> Everything that is times a godzillion, will you destroy and uncreate it all? Right and Wrong, Good and Bad, POD and POC, All 9, Shorts, Boys and Beyonds.

Peace doesn't actually exist as a concept on planet Earth. Where do you see peace occurring? Only in nature is there a sense of peace, and even in that peace, there is violence.

Peace does not exclude violence, because peace is part of oneness, and violence is part of oneness as well. In a sense of peace, there is always a balance of nature, which is a concept that doesn't exist on this planet. In the human race, everybody is supposed to live, everybody is supposed to have peace, everybody is supposed to not suffer, and all that stuff. Is that what the world, the universe, the reality is? Where are you buying a different point of view?

> Everything you have done to buy a different point of view about peace, will you destroy and uncreate all that times a godzillion? Right and Wrong, Good and Bad, POD and POC, All 9, Shorts, Boys and Beyonds.

Peace is one of the things that create us not recognizing that we actually have choice. If you say that the world should be peaceful, meaning that nobody should ever hurt and there should never be any sadness or unhappiness, you're not acknowledging that the people who are having sadness and unhappiness, the people who are experiencing abuse, violence, and all those things, are actually choosing it. And they like it!

Dain: That's not necessarily an easy pill to swallow. It's not necessarily a thing we want to become aware of. That would be very, very surprising.

Gary: When you talk about this stuff to people, their energy goes... zing!

Dain: And your energy goes ziiinnggg!

What physical actualization of the never-ending disease of peace are you not acknowledging, as the perfection of the creation of love, sex, and jealousy as the total and absolute diminishment of the human race into oblivion? Everything that is times a godzillion, will you destroy and uncreate it all? Right and Wrong, Good and Bad, POD and POC, All 9, Shorts, Boys and Beyonds.

Gary: Wow, that is one of the best ones so far! I like that one!

Dain: Wow!

Call Participant: This may be stating the obvious, but I just got that part of the way this distractor implant works is that if you are chasing love, or you're chasing peace, or you're obsessed with jealousy, you cannot be you. You cannot have you.

Gary: In actuality, you can't actually be.

Call Participant: Exactly! It's a fantasy to distract us from us, totally, forever.

Gary: Yes, because as long as you're buying any of these distractor implants as real, you can't actually *be*. That is the purpose of them—to keep you from being—because if you could *be*, you wouldn't choose any of this stuff. You wouldn't see any value in it.

It's like the guy who was saying, "Oh my relationship! I want her back!

I said, "You gave up having a relationship with this woman six years ago. You decided it was over. You decided you didn't want it. You decided it wasn't the right thing for you. And now you're trying to prove that because she is going with somebody else, you have been wronged and you are the victim. You're trying to prove that you actually care about something that you gave up six years ago."

Every one of these distractor implants is designed to create you as the victim. Can you, as an infinite being, truly be a victim? Nope. You have to work at it.

Dain: And notice also, Gary's willingness to have that conversation with the guy. How many of you would have been willing to say that? How absolutely against everything in this reality is it to have a conversation like that? But it was the only thing that would create clarity out of the situation because that was the thing that was going on.

Gary: It was what was true. The guy actually laughed. He said, "Oh my God, you're right."

I said, "Yeah, I know. I'm not right, but I am usually correct." There is a difference between being right and being correct. *Right* means there has to be a wrong; *correct* means anybody else can have a point of view too, and you can still be correct.

> Everything that is times a godzillion, will you destroy and uncreate it all, please? Right and Wrong, Good and Bad, POD and POC, All 9, Shorts, Boys and Beyonds.

Gary: Let's run this again, Dain. I think it is cool.

Dain: Yeah, so do I.

> What physical actualization of the never-ending disease of peace are you not acknowledging as the perfection of the creation of love, sex, and jealousy as the total and absolute diminishment of the human race into oblivion? Everything that is times a godzillion, will you destroy and uncreate it all? Right and Wrong, Good and Bad, POD and POC, All 9, Shorts, Boys and Beyonds.

Gary: Let's change this slightly.

> What physical actualization of the never-ending disease of the lie of peace are you not acknowledging as the perfection of the creation and destruction simultaneously of love, sex, and jealousy as the total and absolute diminishment of the human race into oblivion? Everything that is times a godzillion, will you destroy and uncreate it all? Right and Wrong, Good and Bad, POD and POC, All 9, Shorts, Boys and Beyonds.

Dain: Wow. That is so true. That is so interesting. At the same time people are creating what they think is love, so many of them are also destroying it. Same thing with sex, and same thing with jealousy.

Gary: Right.

Dain: If you have any of those, you're also trying to destroy it. If you have the jealousy part, you're trying to destroy that. If you don't have the right love, you're trying to destroy that in order to try to have something different. If you don't have the right sex, you're trying to destroy that in order to have something different.

Gary: And while you are at it, you also have the creation and destruction of the idea of peace. You have no peace with the idea that this one time of great sex, or great love, or great anything is enough. You always have to have more.

Dain: Which is because we buy the lie of time. We don't realize "If I had it once I am still being it now."

Gary: That it's "I *am* it," not "I have it."

Dain: Wow, and that is what makes us look outside of us for everything—for the love, for the validation of sex.

Gary: For being.

Dain: For our very being—yes, rather than realizing "I am this." Because if you are *something*, you are *everything*. The question is: "What part of that am I choosing to express right now?"

Gary: And "What part of that am I choosing not to express right now?"

Dain: Right.

Gary: Okay, let's try it again.

> What physical actualization of the never-ending disease of the lie of peace are you not acknowledging as the perfection of the creation and the destruction?

We have to change it a little more. It's "the lie and the truth of peace." I love it! Talk about convoluted. You have the lie and truth and you're trying to live both of them.

Dain: And at the same time you have creation and destruction simultaneously and you're trying to live both of those.

> What physical actualization of the never-ending disease of the lie and the truth of peace are you not acknowledging as the perfection of the creation and the destruction simultaneously of love, sex, and jealousy as the total and absolute diminishment of the human race into oblivion? Everything that is times a godzillion, will you destroy and uncreate it all? Right and Wrong, Good and Bad, POD and POC, All 9, Shorts, Boys and Beyonds.

Wow! Holy Tabbouleh, Batman! I used to wonder if we could create a process that could unlock everything. We may have found it!

Gary: That would be funny, wouldn't it?

> What physical actualization of the never-ending disease of the lie and truth of peace are you not acknowledging as the perfection of the creation and the destruction simultaneously of love, sex, and jealousy as the total and absolute diminishment of the human race into oblivion? Everything that is times a godzillion, will you destroy and uncreate it all? Right and Wrong, Good and Bad, POD and POC, All 9, Shorts, Boys and Beyonds.

As we were doing this process, I noticed that for each one of these distractor implants, we go to more of what keeps us from being. This is where we create the opposition to ourselves, the opposition to being and receiving, and the opposition to total awareness of every aspect of our life and living. It is like each one has been built to a greater level. I wonder what the next level will bring.

Dain: Wow.

> What physical actualization of the never-ending disease of the lie and truth of peace are you not acknowledging as the perfection of the creation and the destruction simultaneously of love, sex, and jealousy as the total and absolute diminishment of the human race into oblivion? Everything that is times a godzillion, will you destroy and uncreate it all? Right and Wrong, Good and Bad, POD and POC, All 9, Shorts, Boys and Beyonds.

Gary: My goodness, this is amazing!

Call Participant: Can you explain the word oblivion?

Gary: *Oblivion* is the place in which nothing exists. It is the idea that you can take something that exists and put it into a place where nothing exists. It's the idea that the human race doesn't exist. If we are functioning from the idea that the human race cannot truly exist, that it doesn't really exist, what can we create? Or do we always have constant opposition to creating and generating what is possible as the humans and humanoids we actually are? Does that help?

You will have to listen to that about 2,700 times to get it. I understand that and I am sorry. I wish I could create greater clarity, but if you look in the world, you see that people are always functioning from the point of view that they want to exist and they can't exist. They want to be here but they don't want to be here. They are always in opposition to something in their own world. So many people have been in opposition to some part of who they are and what they are. Does that create a place where they can be who and what they are?

Call Participant: That helps. Thank you very much.

Gary: You're welcome.

Call Participant: I can wrap my head around x amount of this, then there's a piece I need help with. What would it look like in the world if we were like that? Let's say you're in the empty nest stage of your life, and the younger people would like to have families. Is this just setting us up for a brand new paradigm of what relationships would be so that children are growing up with that?

Gary: The one thing that has become real to me is that children have a different point of view than we do, anyway. When I got married to my second wife, she had a fifteen-year-old son. I was in the hot tub with him one night, and I said, "So how does it feel to have a real family?"

He said, "What are you talking about? I have always had a real family. My sister, my mother and I are a real family."

I realized that what we define as a real family creates the limits of what we can have as truth. That's the distractor. We keep trying to generate the weird point of view that a real family is x, y, z. According to whom? According to this reality, according to what we have seen on television, according to what we have read in books, according to comic books, according to all kinds of other things that have nothing to do with our choices and nothing to do with our awareness.

My step-son's awareness was that he, his sister, and his mother were a true family, because they cared about each other, because they were there for each other and because they were willing to encompass each other without judgment.

In that moment I realized, "Wait a minute, my definition of family is not a true definition. It is just my definition." In every aspect of a relationship, you have to look at:

- What is my definition?
- What is the other person's definition?
- What is the real definition?
- What would be a different definition?

We have tried in every aspect of our lives to define what is true and real according to our perspective, or according to someone else's. For example, when I was young and pretty and having sex with everybody, my point of view was: "If I am not the best sex partner you could have, then you should be with somebody else. If they are better than I am, go with them." I didn't get that was not normal. I thought that was the normal point of view someone would have about sex.

Then I was involved with a girl and we had great, fabulous, amazing sex, and she said, "I am leaving you."

I said, "What?"

She said, "The sex is great, but I want a relationship."

I said, "What? I don't get what you're talking about."

She said, "You're better in bed than this guy, but this guy will make a commitment of his life to me."

I said, "What?" Because for me, it was about love, sex, jealousy, and peace. I had a sense of peace when I had sex with her. I didn't have that with anyone else. She had a sense of peace when she had sex with me, which she didn't have with anyone else, but because that didn't fit with the idea of relationship in this reality, it couldn't exist for her.

And for me it was, "I don't get what you're talking about."

It couldn't exist because it wasn't something she could define according to somebody's point of view, which didn't even have to be hers. And she definitely could not define it according to her reality. All these distractor implants are defining your reality—not by your awareness, but by somebody else's.

Dain: Another way to answer your questions is to ask: "Will this change the paradigm of relationship that is available?" I would say the answer is yes; there is a possibility at least. A lot of people get into relationships so they can get the love they think they are lacking or the sex that they think they are lacking. Yet they go into opposition because there are many people who say, "Yes, I would like the sex, and I'd like the love, but I don't really want to be committed or tied down." Well, how are you going to get that?

Right now it doesn't exist in this reality. And in truth, the only way to have the peace is to have all of you and not require someone. Then you can be in relationship or have sex or copulation with somebody, and it can be a contribution to your life. When you're always looking to other people's reality to find yours, there isn't the possibility for peace to exist.

Some of the younger generation, teenagers and college-aged people, are bringing different paradigms to the planet right now. They are doing things differently, and that is making a lot of older people uncomfortable, because the younger people are doing relationship, sex, and copulation without necessarily having nurturing, caring, or work involved. They are trying something different, which means something is changing. We may not be at the place yet, but something is definitely changing on the planet.

Gary: Because you guys are doing these distractor implants, the chance of something greater showing up is improved. I am grateful to you for being on these calls. And I am grateful that we actually decided to do these calls.

put on a loop

Dain:

> What physical actualization of the never-ending disease of the lie and the truth of peace are you not acknowledging as the perfection of the creation and the destruction simultaneously of love, sex, and jealousy as the total and absolute diminishment of the human race into oblivion? Everything that is times a godzillion, will you destroy and uncreate it all? Right and Wrong, Good and Bad, POD and POC, All 9, Shorts, Boys and Beyonds.

Call Participant: Dain, whatever you said before really hit me, and at the same time, I didn't understand you. It was as if you spoke Chinese, yet it was really profound. I would love if you could repeat it.

Dain: Thank you. You're going to need to listen to the replay.

Gary: About 500 times.

Call Participant: Okay.

Dain: We look through other people's realities to try to find our reality and to try to find us.

I did a class a while ago on unlocking and finding the true happiness of you. The class was based on some work I was doing with Gary. It was very interesting to me, because I realized that I was doing something and that pretty much everybody else was doing it too. I had a basic question in my head, which was:

- What can I be that is different than me to find the happiness I truly be?
- What can I be that is not me that will allow me to find the happiness, I truly be?

But it can also be:

- What can I be that is different than me to find the happiness, I truly be?
- What can I be that is not me that will allow me to find the peace I truly be?

This is where people have been functioning from. If you just ask those questions and then POC and POD it, you will start to come out of the place where you are trying to do that. We are already us, yet it doesn't seem to be working. Since the time we were conceived, we have looked for what we could be other than us that would allow us to finally be happy and peaceful here. We're really good at looking through other people's realities and trying to mimic them, trying to duplicate them, but it doesn't fit us, and it doesn't work because the only thing that will give you the peace and happiness of you, is having all of you with no judgment.

Gary: We think peace is a part of us. P-i-e-c-e is not p-e-a-c-e. We keep trying to look for the piece of us that is missing, as though once we have a relationship, we will have a sense of peace and the whole of us by having the sense of peace that we get when the other piece of us starts to show up.

> Everything that is times a godzillion, will you destroy and uncreate it all? Right and Wrong, Good and Bad, POD and POC, All 9, Shorts, Boys and Beyonds.

When I heard there were distractor implants, I got it. I'd say, "Okay, that's a distractor. POC and POD that." I didn't realize that the majority of the people don't function from that point of view. They're always trying to look at *why* is it so, or *how* is it so, or *what* is so.

Dain: They think that if you can finally figure it out, you won't be doing it anymore.

Gary: Yeah.

Dain: No, it will just give yourself more reason to judge you for not having already changed it.

Gary:
> What physical actualization of the never-ending disease of the lie and truth of peace are you not acknowledging as the perfection of the creation and the destruction simultaneously of love, sex, and jealousy as the total and absolute diminishment of the human race into oblivion? Everything that is times a godzillion, will you destroy and uncreate it all? Right and Wrong, Good and Bad, POD and POC, All 9, Shorts, Boys and Beyonds.

We have to add something else: "into oblivion and annihilation of total being."

> What physical actualization of the never-ending disease of the lie and truth of peace are you not acknowledging as the perfection of the creation and the destruction simultaneously of love, sex, and jealousy as the total and absolute diminishment of the human race into oblivion and annihilation of being? Everything that is times a godzillion, will you destroy and uncreate it all? Right and Wrong, Good and Bad, POD and POC, All 9, Shorts, Boys and Beyonds.

It's like we are always trying to prove that we are part of the human race. And we do love, sex, jealousy, and peace as a way of proving that. You fall in love with somebody, so you try to create a sense of peace within the structure of your life based on the peace of having the other part of you, a piece of you that is missing.

You try to create that, and you end up in a place where you are trying to hold it together. You're trying to keep the jealousy in existence. You think that if you can hold that fixed point of view in existence, nothing will change. But it's all a distractor implant. It's designed to eliminate you from being in the first place. Amazing.

Dain: Brilliant, darling, brilliant!

Gary:

> Everywhere you bought that crock of shit, and everything that is times a godzillion, will you destroy and uncreate it all? Right and Wrong, Good and Bad, POD and POC, All 9, Shorts, Boys and Beyonds.

> What physical actualization of the never-ending disease of the lie and truth of peace, are you not acknowledging as the perfection of the creation and the destruction simultaneously of love, sex, and jealousy as the total and absolute diminishment of the human race into oblivion and annihilation of total being? Everything that is times a godzillion, will you destroy and uncreate it all? Right and Wrong, Good and Bad, POD and POC, All 9, Shorts, Boys and Beyonds.

Call Participant: You said sex is when you're walking tall, strutting your stuff, and being all of you, and that it feels amazing. It seems like I allow something to come in and I twist it or I contract. I go into judgment or buy other people's judgment. Can you talk about that?

Gary: That's called extrapolation—and that is called distractor implants!

Dain: Every distractor implant is designed to loop into or around another distractor implant or another point of limitation. It's like a Mobius strip—but it's not just one. Do you know what a Mobius strip is? It's the infinity sign. It's like a Mobius strip made out of Mobius strips.

Call Participant: Yes.

Dain: Imagine a Mobius strip made out of Mobius strips. No matter where you join it, it's designed so you always loop back into the Mobius strip of limitation that gets created from the distractor implants themselves. And the reason we are doing all of them is because…

Gary: They are all contributory to one another. They are all contributory to the limitations of you. They are not a creator of possibilities.

Dain: They loop back towards each other. There are a lot of spiritual and self-help practices you have done in this lifetime and other lifetimes, and they take one piece of a distractor implant scenario. For example, how many people do you know who are into love? "Love will save us. Love will set us free. Love is God. Love is the greatest thing in the world." These people are disconnected from reality. They want everything to be love because in some lifetime, they belonged to a cult or created a cult that said, "Love is the way to set us free." But unfortunately, because these things keep looping back to each other, it is not possible to create freedom from that venue.

So you'll have people who think love is the way out. It's not nearly all-encompassing enough, because as soon as they get clear in the area of love—and usually they are not clear, they are usually highly concluded—they run into the other distractor implants that send them right back into everything they were limited on. It's based on love, or now it's about jealousy, or now it's about sex, which is why so many spiritual religious teachings are "If you truly want to be spiritual, cut out sex and stop enjoying your body." Except that doesn't work either, because it doesn't include all of you.

We are looking to get you to a place where you can have freedom with all the energies and possibilities that are available rather than getting twisted back into the spiral that is created if you hop on the train of any of these distractor implants. Does that make sense?

Call Participant: Yeah, thanks. I want to be able to be that sex and that joyfulness, and I get that running the clearing and being aware will allow that—because I really bind to the judgment.

Gary: That is what a distractor implant is designed to do. It's designed to draw you into the judgment, not into the awareness. If you realize that, when you have sex with somebody who is really great to have sex with, you want all of your friends to experience that greatness too. When I was doing sex, drugs, and rock and roll—my point of view was "Well, how do I get my friends to experience how great this person is to have sex with?"

My friends would say "You want me to do what?"

I'd say, "She is fabulous in bed. How can you miss this?"

They would say, "Are you crazy?"

I'd say, "What do you mean?"

They would ask, "You want to share this person?"

I'd say, "Yeah, and if you're good, I would like to share you, too."

They would say, "You're sick." That is when I stopped sharing.

Dain: That, unfortunately, is the same sort of the experience a lot of us have had in whatever way it occurred that made us stop sharing and stop being the generosity of us, which is part of what really makes life joyful.

We have spent so much of our time and energy cutting off what was true about us to try to make what these distractor implants say is true.

As we were growing up, we cut off one finger, and then a toe, and another toe, and then we cut off our butt cheek. And we wonder why it seems like we are functioning with less than all of our capacities. We think that is where we have to go and that is what we have to do because that is what everyone else seems to think is true.

> Everything that is times a godzillion, will you destroy and uncreate it, please? Right and Wrong, Good and Bad, POD and POC, All 9, Shorts, Boys and Beyonds.

> What physical actualization of the never-ending disease of the lie and truth of peace are you not acknowledging as the perfection of the creation and the destruction simultaneously of love, sex, and jealousy as the total and absolute diminishment of the human race into oblivion and annihilation of total being? Everything that is times a godzillion, will you destroy and uncreate it all? Right and Wrong, Good and Bad, POD and POC, All 9, Shorts, Boys and Beyonds.

Call Participant: I am getting clear on how these three distractor implants work together. It's like you just can't take one. They're all together. Can you talk about sex and love as a distractor implant? And can you extrapolate a little bit more on the energy of "falling in love" and "then having sex" and having it be like a drug?

Dain: In the first distractor implant call, we talked about how anger is actually potency, and potency is actually the reality, but when you align and agree with some part of the potency, the anger, which is a very similar vibration, but just "slightly off," ends up "trapping" you.

It's the same with peace. Peace is what is true for you in much the same way potency is what's true. But if you align and agree with any aspect of it, you are setting yourself up to be screwed up by the distractor implant of love, sex, and jealousy.

As for "falling in love," what if that is actually who you be?

Gary: The idea of "falling in love" is the distractor implant of this thing. It's something you "fall into." It's not something you're aware of.

Dain: And it's not something you already are and can choose to be.

Call Participant: Yeah. It's as if it's not a natural state. Like when you feel it, it's like "This is who I am." It's like it resonates. Yeah.

Dain: Rather than *being*, this distractor implant puts it into *feeling*. And a feeling is a transient state, which you know is going to go away. But if it is something you *be*, it can't ever be taken away from you.

Call Participant: What is that energy when you're so full of love that you just have to say, "I love you"?

Dain: Is it that you are so full of love? Or are you actually full of being that has been misidentified and misapplied? Have you noticed that any time that you are being so much, there is a compulsion to share it?

Call Participant: Right!

Dain: I always wanted to share the things I came across, the awarenesses I had, and the spaces of being I found were available, especially after I started Access Consciousness, but even before Access. I'd be having an amazing day when I was running along the beach, and no matter how fast I ran, nothing could get me winded. I'd be sprinting, I'd be having a great time, and then I would run past somebody who looked at me. I would want to share this energy with their body because their body had very little of it. And as soon as I tried to share it with them, my universe would contract to the same size as theirs.

When you share—and I think this is part of this distractor implant thing that occurs with love—if your universe is larger than the other person's, you have to contract to the size of their universe in this particular area in order to give it to them.

This takes you out of being the expansiveness that is greater than they're aware of and it puts you into trying to be something smaller than you were in order to give it to them. You are no longer any greater than they are. You are out of the amazing space you were being.

Gary:
> Everything that is and brought up times a godzillion, will you destroy and uncreate it all? Right and Wrong, Good and Bad, POD and POC, All 9, Shorts, Boys and Beyonds.

Dain: I am sorry for the longwinded nature of that.

Call Participant: No Dain, it was brilliant the way you danced through that. Can it go both ways? When you truly acknowledge the energy that is, does it expand?

Dain: Yes, but in a place where you don't need to share it.

Call Participant: You just be it. You just be what it be?

FEELING

Dain: Guys, please get this. This is so big. Most people will never let themselves see it or acknowledge it. Anytime you say, "I feel I need to share this" or "I feel" to something," POC and POD all that and ask: "What's the awareness I am having that's greater than this feeling?" In every feeling there is an awareness you're not willing to have. We have been saying this for twelve years, but nobody wants to hear it. People want to say, "I feel so full of love." No, you are actually aware that you be something that is greater.

Gary: Here is something I would like you to do: Take somebody you care about, somebody you truly care about, and make that intimate feeling bigger than the universe. Is that feeling of caring greater than you will actually acknowledge?

Dain: Yes.

Gary: That is the level of caring and love you actually have. We keep trying to diminish it to this reality's version of what love is. That is the oblivion and the lack of being that we keep trying to create from.

Dain: Even your dogs know it!

Gary: Yeah!

Call Participant: It seems to me that sometimes when people fall in love, it's really about "I have found the answer. Now I don't have to search anymore!" It seems the opposite of what you are talking about. It's almost like a diminishment.

Gary: Well, if you are falling in love, you're falling to a diminished state.

Dain: And you're falling into conclusion. The thing that goes with this is a contextual reality, where people want to fit, they want to benefit, they want to win, and they want to not lose. Falling in love fills all those bills, except it cuts off your willingness to be anything else, anything greater than that.

You come to the conclusion "I finally found the one! I finally found the answer! I finally fit, I finally benefit. I'm finally winning. I finally am not a loser anymore." You try to stop there, which keeps you from moving forward, but you, as a being, need to expand or you're contracting and dying.

We all try to conclude things based on this reality. We say, "Ooh let me find a nice soft space and end up there!" When you do that, you're always falling into less than you.

It's kind of like the sex aspect of this distractor implant. If you get the way it feels when you are flirting with somebody and they're flirting with you—hopefully all of you know what that is like—and you get this "living" in your body that is a state of energy that should be available for your body all the time. We tend to think, "Oh, this is about somebody else!" or "Oh, I only have this when I have sex." Well, what if it could be even greater, whether or not you have sex or copulation or somebody to copulate with?

Call Participant: Is this what you were saying before? When we have that experience, when we have the energy that is in our body—a lot of times it happens when we are with somebody else—we identify it as something that we can only experience with somebody else? Are you saying that once you have that experience, you are it?

Gary: If you are *having an experience* of it, you're actually not *being* it. When you look for the experience of something, you are looking for a way to validate what you have decided, concluded, and confirmed is true that may not be true.

Dain: The only reason you could have what you call "the experience" is because you *are* that already. It's only because you be it that you can have the experience, and when you go to "Wow, I have this *experience,"* instead of, "Wow, I *am this*," you're taking yourself out of the place of being it and into the need of someone else to fulfill it or to bring it to you.

You're also going into needing someone else, as though if you don't have that person, you won't have these wonderful aspects of being and being embodied that you are now having and getting to be. Does that make sense?

Call Participant: Thank you. That is such a huge difference!

Call Participant: When we are being intimate, when we are having copulation or sex, how is it that we can do it just to have fun? If we are looking for that outside of us, what is the value of having sex with other people who are already being that energy?

Dain: You are making the assumption "If I can be all this, why do I need somebody else?" It's not that you *need* somebody else. If I can be all of this, I need a body! You don't *need* a body. You created a body so you could play with it, have fun in it, enjoy it, and experience things that you couldn't experience nearly as easily without one.

Gary: You don't get to experience it and enjoy it because you don't have a sense of peace with your body. You don't have a sense of love and sex. You know jealousy with your body. You have all this other stuff you think you're supposed to have based on whose point of view?

Dain: It ain't your point of view. It's somebody else's.

Call Participant: (Laughing)

Dain:

> What physical actualization of the never-ending disease of the lie and truth of peace, are you not acknowledging as the perfection of the creation and the destruction simultaneously of love, sex, and jealousy as the total and absolute diminishment of the human race into oblivion and annihilation of total being? Everything that is times a godzillion, will you destroy and uncreate it all? Right and Wrong, Good and Bad, POD and POC, All 9, Shorts, Boys and Beyonds.

Call Participant: There are many courses and conferences around the world that focus on learning to love everyone on the planet, spreading the love, and so on. Is this version of love a distractor implant?

Gary: It is always a distractor implant, because if they can get you to focus on love, you won't notice the fact that they are killing you. Okay, next question.

Dain: Don't you want to say any more on that?

Gary: No, I have said all I want to say.

Participants: (Laughing)

Gary: For years everybody has told me, "It's all about the love, all about the love, all about the love." Has the love grown? No! So how can it be about the love if the love hasn't grown? Things haven't gotten better. There hasn't been a different possibility out in the world. I personally have not seen a great shift or change in that. So for me, "It's all about the love" is of what value? It's the idea that there is something greater than you that you have not even noticed yet.

Dain: Good point. There is something greater than you that you haven't even noticed yet. How much of that is perpetrated on you by so many of the techniques out there and so many of the people saying, "We've got the right answers. This is the way to do it."

If there is truly something greater than you that you haven't noticed yet, when you get the awareness that there is something greater that you haven't yet chosen to be, it should make you feel lighter, as in "Wow, there is more that I can be!" That's not where this stuff is coming from. It's more like "There is something greater than you, and you're not it."

Gary: I love the "you're not it" part. That's sounds so good.

Call Participant: It seems that there is a pervasive point of view out there that to grow, you have to be in a partnership, because that is going to show you what you need to work on. And you can practice your communication if you're in a partnership or relationship.

Gary: Thank you for the greatest crock of shit I have ever heard in my life. What part of your infinite being, if you don't have infinite awareness, are you not acknowledging? I am sorry folks, I love you all, but you're just buying a crock of shit with chocolate on it. It still tastes like shit—so don't eat it. There is a whole universe out there where people are saying, "It's this, it's this, it's this." You focus on "this, this, and this," and how does your life work? Next question.

Call Participant: My impression is that the more I become aware of me, the more the relationship becomes more joyful—lighter.

Gary: Yeah, because it becomes about possibility, choice, question, and contribution—and not about what it is *supposed* to be. All these distractor implants are designed to give you what is *supposed to be*, because you will choose what is *supposed to be* and fail, and then you have to go into judgment of you. If you don't have to judge you, what other choices are available?

Call Participant: Has jealousy always been in the world? In historical stories, it seems that there is always something about jealousy. Are there not parts of the world or a generation in which there was not so much jealousy?

Gary: No, there has always been jealousy in one form or another. As we've said, jealousy is about not having things change. That is the purpose of jealousy—to not have things change. It's about not having the physical structure of anyone's reality change. This is not the same as envy, which people have misidentified and misapplied as jealousy. *Envy* is wanting what somebody else has. *Jealousy* is "I don't want it to change."

Most of us misidentify and misapply that we are jealous when we actually want what somebody else has. We think that what they have would be more fun than what we seem to have, which is less fun than what we would have if we were willing to have it.

> Everything that is times a godzillion, will you destroy and uncreate it all? Right and Wrong, Good and Bad, POD and POC, All 9, Shorts, Boys and Beyonds.

Call Participant: I asked my mother to tell me about sex when I was nineteen. She blushed and wouldn't look at me. She told me that we would talk when I got married. I lost my virginity with my first boyfriend who is now my husband, and not in a very gentle way. I hated that, and I have never enjoyed sex. I always felt like a sex object.

Gary: If you're doing sex from the place of the distractor implant universe, it is never about enjoying your body. It's about being an object. You look at sex from being an object and having a judgment of sex. Definitely.

> How many "definite judgments" do you have about sex that keep you from enjoying your body totally? Everything that is times a godzillion, will you destroy and uncreate it all? Right and Wrong, Good and Bad, POD and POC, All 9, Shorts, Boys and Beyonds.

Call Participant: How is sex a distractor implant? I recognize that when you don't like sex, it distracts you from being present. But what if you want it all the time or it's like a drug? Can you speak to that?

Dain: Well, that is the sexuality of things—it is like a drug that takes you away from you. It's where you want it all the time, where you need it all the time. This goes back to the idea that sexuality is a place where you're not able to receive all of you. When sex becomes a drug, it's "Oh wow! I felt so good when I had sex with this person! I feel so good when I have people to have sex with! I feel so good when they have sex with me."

Sexuality is being invoked in that scenario, not the *sexualness* that takes you beyond the distractor implant of sex. What are you not being in that scenario that if you were willing to be it, would change your relationship to the situation?

Dain: Does that help?

Call Participant: Yes, and I feel like there are two things in play, like the Mobius strips or quantum particulates.

Gary: Only if you create two things that are in opposition to each other can you make yourself in opposition to yourself.

Call Participant: So how does that work?

Gary: Truth, do you like sex?

Call Participant: Yes.

Gary: Yeah, so what is going to happen? Only if you keep you in opposition to yourself can you keep in existence the place where you are not capable of being. All these distractor implants, and the other side of them, make you think you have to have them, and if you don't have them, you're wrong. They keep you in a constant state of opposition from actually being you. You like sex, and if somebody actually enjoys sex, do you and your body get turned on?

Call Participant: Yes.

Gary: Yes. The majority of the world uses sex to create judgment in order to create their sexual excitation, which is very different from what we're talking about. You've got to get to the point where you ask, "Do I like sex? Yes or no?"

Call Participant: Yes.

Gary: Okay, then you're going need to be turned on by somebody else's body being turned on. That is sex to you. And if somebody does not use judgment to create sexual excitation, you're probably going to find that you and your body are going to get more turned on than ninety-nine of the people out there.

Call Participant: Yes.

Gary: So the good news is, you're just a slut.

Call Participant: (Laughing) I guess my question is about being present in the intensity of slutdom.

Gary: Yes, I understand. You're saying that if you walk into these distractor implants, you're going to feel a heaviness and a contraction. That is the place where you walk into the distractor implant instead of walking into the possibly that the intensity of awareness gives you.

Call Participant: So it's more about the intensity of awareness that I know is possible?

Gary: Yes, and you have to be willing to ask: "Is this an intensity that is expansive? Or is this an intensity that is contractive?" If it is contractive, it is a distractor implant. If it's expansive, it is not.

Call Participant: I just need to get bigger.

Gary: Yep.

Call Participant: Cool.

Depression

Call Participant: I was surprised that sadness and depression are not distractor implants. Depression, especially, has a Mobius strip quality to it. I just recently came out from under an episode of depression and I remembered that it is sometimes referred to as anger turned inward.

Gary: Is that a truth? Or is that a lie that is told to try to make you believe that depression is real for you? Depression is usually your awareness of somebody else's stuff. Truth, did you grow up with somebody who was depressed all the time?

Call Participant: No.

Dain: Is that true?

Gary: You just lied to me.

Call Participant: Well, my mom wasn't depressed all the time. She had some depression she recognized later, but she didn't realize it was depression while I was growing up.

Gary: No. She didn't acknowledge it as depression while you were growing up. She was depressed her whole frigging life. And she probably bought it from somebody she knew who was depressed.

Call Participant: Probably.

Dain: Did you notice she just got lighter when you said that?

Gary: The reality is that you grew up with somebody who was depressed, and you spent your whole life trying to take it away from her. Yes or No?

Call Participant: *I don't actually remember that, but I got a yes.*

Gary: It's not about the memory; it's about the awareness you have to function from. When you're around someone who is depressed and you try to take it away from them and they won't let you, you spend your entire life trying to take depression away from others. And it's never going to work.

> Everything you have done to try to take other people's sadness and depression and make it yours, will you destroy and uncreate all that times a godzillion, please? Right and Wrong, Good and Bad, POD and POC, All 9, Shorts, Boys and Beyonds.

I want you to get this—you're basically happy. When you take on other people's sadness and depression, how is that working for you?

Call Participant: *(Laughing)*

Gary: That might have applied to a few others of you out there. You might have this hideous terrible problem called "I am basically happy."

> Everywhere you have had that problem, will you destroy and uncreate it all? Right and Wrong, Good and Bad, POD and POC, All 9, Shorts, Boys and Beyonds.

Dain: People will tell you, "Depression is anger turned inward" or "it's this and it's this." They are not looking from a place of lightness of being that actually is. They are looking from this reality's point of view.

Gary: They are not trying to question. They are trying to come to conclusion and answer.

Dain: As though if they can get the right conclusion, they can help change the problem. What if depression is not actually a problem? What if depression for you is like the ADD, ADHD, OCD, and autism the kids we work with have? We let them know it is not a problem; it's a greatness this reality doesn't recognize.

Gary: If you would actually acknowledge the greatness you have and the ability to be happy, you would actually have to be happy. So give it up.

Dain: And if you had to acknowledge that you are more aware than the people who are telling you how screwed up you are, that would be really bad, because then you wouldn't have to buy into it.

Call Participant: I don't have people telling me that I am screwed up. I just tell myself that.

Gary: Well, that is the nice part about it. You can tell yourself that all day long; other people can only tell you once a day.

It's Okay to Be Happy

Call Participant: I am getting waves of nausea and I feel like crying and I don't know why. Can you do a clearing with me please?

Gary: Darling, darling, does that actually belong to you?

Call Participant: No, I can just feel it.

Gary: Just because you can feel it doesn't mean it's real. It's the same terrible problem we talked about with the last question. It's called "You are actually happy."

Call Participant: (Laughing)

Gary: The good news is that because you can feel other people's unhappiness, you assume it must be yours.

Call Participant: You're right, thank you.

Gary: You're welcome.

> All of you who keep trying to make yourself as unhappy as everyone else is, so you can be as unhappy as they have decided they ought to be, so you can be like other people, so you can be as miserable as everyone else who thinks it's right to be miserable, so you don't have to be as different as you really are and as happy all the time when everybody else is miserable, and so you don't

have to tell them how happy you are, will you destroy and uncreate it all? Right and Wrong, Good and Bad, POD and POC, All 9, Shorts, Boys and Beyonds.

Dain:

What physical actualization of the never-ending disease of the lie and truth of peace, are you not acknowledging as the perfection of the creation and the destruction simultaneously of love, sex, and jealousy as the total and absolute diminishment of the human race into oblivion and annihilation of total being? Everything that is times a godzillion, will you destroy and uncreate it all please? Right and Wrong, Good and Bad, POD and POC, All 9, Shorts, Boys and Beyonds.

Call Participant: I've found that it's often the humanoids who have depression. They don't know it's okay to be them. They cut off this part of themselves.

Gary: It's like it's a jungle, and it's okay to be happy.

Call Participant: Yeah, and what if you could be you, and chose for you, and not try to fit in their life? Wow, really? Okay!

Gary:

It is more fun to be unhappy than it is to be happy. It must be so—because everyone else is doing it. Why, shouldn't you? Everything that is times a godzillion, will you destroy and uncreate it all? Right and Wrong, Good and Bad, POD and POC, All 9, Shorts, Boys and Beyonds.

Dain:

What physical actualization of the never-ending disease of the lie and truth of peace, are you not acknowledging as the perfection of the creation and the destruction simultaneously of love, sex, and jealousy as the total and absolute diminishment of the human race into oblivion and annihilation of total being? Everything that is times a godzillion, will you destroy and uncreate it all? Right and Wrong, Good and Bad, POD and POC, All 9, Shorts, Boys and Beyonds.

Call Participant: How can I have love as a choice—not as a necessity?

Gary: That is not a question. It is a statement with a question mark attached. What you should ask instead is: "Am I doing this from necessity—or am I doing this from choice?" If you love somebody from choice, not from necessity, would there be a different possibility in your life? Absolutely not … or maybe there would be!

Call Participant: When are sex and love a distractor implant and when are they not?

Gary: Sex and love are always a distractor implant because it is never about "Oh, would I like to do this," or "Would I not like to do this?" or "What do I need to get out of this?" That it is a choice. You've got to ask: "Is this necessity or a choice?" "Is it a necessity for this person to call me in the morning? Yes or no?" No? Okay good! "That was fun! Thanks so much. See you later—bye bye."

Call Participant: How does that show up and take us out of awareness? I recently met a guy. My body seems really turned on around him, but when I am away from him, I can't be bothered to stay in touch.

Gary: That's called good sex. You're right. Don't worry about it. He's very single minded, and all of his focus is on the physicality of who you might be to each other. Ignore him and enjoy the sex.

Call Participant: Can you talk about my particular situation and how it is or is not a distractor implant?

Gary: It's not a distractor implant if you are just enjoying it and you don't have to think about it again. If you have to think about it all the time, it is a distractor implant. Please get that: If you have to think about it all the time it's a distractor implant. If you have to think about it all the time, it is a distractor implant. If you have to think about it all the time, it's a distractor implant.

If you have to think about it all the time, it's a distractor implant. And if you don't feel any energy, you are in the distractor implant.

Call Participant: I like sex and I am not willing to give it up.

Gary: Who said you have to?

Dain: Exactly.

Call Participant: How do I have sex as part of my life without having it be a distractor?

Gary: Just like you're having it. If you can say, "Thank you very much! See you later!" then you are not doing it from a distractor implant.

> Everything that brought up for everybody else, will you destroy and uncreate it all times a godzillion? Right and Wrong, Good and Bad, POD and POC, All 9, Shorts, Boys and Beyonds.

Call Participant: I heard one of you say that there are hundreds of ways a person can love someone. That helped me understand that there is no way my mom could ever love me the way I "needed" to be loved. So I have looked for it from others, I have tried to love myself, mostly by reducing how much I judge myself. Is there anything else I can do?

Gary: Distractor implants create judgment. That is the sole purpose of them. If you are doing love of self, sex with self, peace with self, jealousy of self, or jealousy with anybody, you're not actually being. The purpose of all distractor implants is to keep you from being, and love is one of the things that keeps you from being, because if you were being, you would have only gratitude; you would not love.

> Everything that is times a godzillion, will you destroy and uncreate it all? Right and Wrong, Good and Bad, POD and POC, All 9, Shorts, Boys and Beyonds.

Call Participant: I have a distractor called "but." It distracts me all the time. Could "but" be a distractor helper?

Gary: "But" is a justification for everything you are choosing. It's what you use to justify what you're choosing as though justifying what you're choosing will get you to the awareness of what you are choosing, as though what you are choosing is right and "but" is the way in which you become right and never wrong.

Dain: I have to say the obvious here: If your head is so up your "but," it could be a distraction to knowing where you are going.

Participants: (Laughing)

Dain: I just had to say that, sorry.

> What physical actualization of the never-ending disease of the lie and truth of peace, are you not acknowledging as the perfection of the creation and the destruction simultaneously of love, sex, and jealousy as the total and absolute diminishment of the human race into oblivion and annihilation of total being? Everything that is times a godzillion, will you destroy and uncreate it all? Right and Wrong, Good and Bad, POD and POC, All 9, Shorts, Boys and Beyonds.

Call Participant: I have noticed that when my husband looks at other women and thinks they are attractive, I sometimes get jealous. How can I change this?

Gary: When that occurs, take him home and fuck him blind immediately. That is how you change the situation.

Dain: But, before you do that, say, "This is what Gary and Dain recommended." And then he will like us too.

Participants: (Laughing)

Call Participant: I would like to have this situation as an interesting point of view, but when this happens, I compare myself with the other women—and I am always the loser. I feel ugly and inadequate, and I hate the women I have decided are prettier, sexier, and smarter.

Gary: There's something you're not getting. Your husband is using other women to stimulate himself. He is a stimulator. If you want to make this work for you, when he stimulates himself, ask: "Would you like to have sex with that one? Would you like to have sex with that one? Would you like to have sex with that one? Would you like to go home and have sex?"

Yeah—because he can't have them and he already has you. He would much rather have you because he is already with you. Girl, you are an idiot.

Dain: There is one more thing you might want to look at. It may seem a little weird, but try it on and see if you can get some awareness on this. How much of this is that you would actually like to have sex with the women he is looking at, and you feel excluded from that? In other words, there is an energy of competition that gets sped up when you don't acknowledge that somewhere in your world, their body or who they are or how they look is stimulating to you too.

I know that can sound like a weird one, but it's one of the big aspects of sex as a distractor implant. You look at them and say, "They have a female body and I am not gay and this doesn't apply and I can't go there, blah, blah, blah."

Guess, what? With anybody who has attraction, who is pulling energy, who has a sensualness to them, if you're alive, your body is going to get turned on.

Gary: And if you ain't alive, you ain't gonna get turned on, so you might as well kill yourself.

Dain: The sex you're not willing to have with somebody creates some of the biggest walls and barriers when you don't allow yourself to indulge it or acknowledge it. When you indulge in something, you become aware of the energy that would be created by the choice you make. See if it is there. Try it. Acknowledge that it could be there. Then ask: "What would it be like if it was there?" Indulge it for a few minutes and notice whether you are willing to have those barriers lowered, and whether you feel like more of you.

Gary: Well, I hate to say it folks, but we've run out of time.

You don't *have* to have love, sex, jealousy, and peace. You can actually have question, choice, possibility, and contribution.

> What contribution is the distractor implant to your life, and what diminishment of your life is it? Is the contribution to the diminishment of you what you really want to have? Everything that is times a godzillion, will you destroy and uncreate it all? Right and Wrong, Good and Bad, POD and POC, All 9, Shorts, Boys and Beyonds.

I hope this helps you all. Please get clear that these distractor implants are not in your best interest. They are all designed to diminish you and to make you judge you.

If you are going into anything like love, sex, jealousy, or peace from the point of view of judging you for not being, doing, having or generating them, you are functioning from distractor implants. POC and POD that shit and move on.

Dain: We have given you a lot of ponder in this call, so please, go back and listen again, because it will change a huge amount of stuff for you.

Gary: And keep running these processes. Put them on a loop!

Chapter Five
Life, Living, Death, and Reality

Gary: Hello everyone. Today we're going to talk about the distractor implants life, living, death, and reality.

Life

Life is what you keep pursuing on planet Earth as though if you get it right, you will have a life. But here's the thing about trying to get something right: you have to be in judgment 24/7.

> Everywhere you have looked for life as though if you can get it right, you will have a life, as though that is what you really want and it will work out right. Everything that is times a godzillion, will you destroy and uncreate it all? Right and Wrong, Good and Bad, POD and POC, All 9, Shorts, Boys and Beyonds.

Apparently you all have been doing that pretty well. You've been trying to find your life through the right and wrong of it.

> What physical actualization of the terminal and eternal disease of generation, creation, and institution are you not acknowledging as the definitive limitation of life on planet Earth? Everything that is times a godzillion, will you destroy and uncreate it all? Right and Wrong, Good and Bad, POD and POC, All 9, Shorts, Boys and Beyonds.

> How many of you realize that in trying to have a life, you have been trying to define what having a life is without having a clue

about what having a life is, while pretending that if you could figure it out, you would know what life was? But you would still not be having a life because you are not bothering to generate, create, or institute it most of the time. And that is what true life and living are. They are the capacity for generative, creative, and institutive choices. Everything that is times a godzillion, will you destroy and uncreate it all? Right and Wrong, Good and Bad, POD and POC, All 9, Shorts, Boys and Beyonds.

Call Participant: What are definitive limitations, Gary?

Gary: *Definitive limitations* is trying to define everything. "I will have a life if I have x, y z." "I will have a life if I have enough money." "I will have a life if I have a perfect relationship." "I will have a life if I have a good relationship." "I will have a life if I have a relationship at all." "I will have a life if I have a good business." "I will have a life if I am doing what everybody else is doing." It's all the *ifs* we use to try to define what a life is rather than asking: "What really do I have as a choice, a question, a possibility, or a contribution here?" That is another universe.

Call Participant: Are limitations something we define?

Gary: Yes, in order to have a limitation, we have to define it.

Call Participant: That is the first time I have heard you say that, Gary. Thank you!

Gary: Well, I have said forever that definition, by definition alone, is limitation.

Call Participant: It's the first time I have heard it. It makes sense, because if you have a limitation, it is actually a definition.

Gary: Yes. To have a limitation of any kind, you have to be able to define something. Whatever you define becomes the limitation you cannot change.

Call Participant: My whole life is limitations! Definitions of what I think my life can be, could be, can't be, will be, and won't be.

Gary: Yes, and it has nothing to do with true choice.

What physical actualization of the terminal and eternal disease of generation, creation, and institution are you not acknowledging as the definitive limitations of life on planet Earth? Everything that is times a godzillion, will you destroy and uncreate it all? Right and Wrong, Good and Bad, POD and POC, All 9, Shorts, Boys and Beyonds.

What physical actualization of the terminal and equivocal disease of choice, question, possibility, and contribution are you not acknowledging as the determining factors of living according to the rules of living on planet Earth? Everything that is times a godzillion, will you destroy and uncreate it all? Right and Wrong, Good and Bad, POD and POC, All 9, Shorts, Boys and Beyonds.

People define themselves by a thousand different things. I was on a plane this morning, and some people were saying, "Oh, you can go ahead of me."

I said, "I don't need to go ahead of you. I am fine." I realized they were seeing me as older than they were, so they assumed I needed to go first. Then there were other people who decided that since they had come out of business class, they needed to go before I did. "Excuse me, who made you God just because you were in business class?"

These are the definitions by which people determine what they are going to choose in life, as the determining factors for life.

Call Participant: Is life a limitation, and living a definitive energy, Gary?

Gary: When you try to define what is going to create your life, are you actually in the process of generating and creating?

Call Participant: No.

Gary: No. You are in the process of defining it, which validates the limitations you have. It validates the limitations you are experiencing and does not allow you to choose something different.

Call Participant: It keeps me in limitation-ville.

Gary: Yes, it's like where we live is the definition of our social class—if we have definition of social class. We have definition of what we drive. All these things are defining factors for determining how we make other people see us, which ain't necessarily true.

Call Participant: Right.

Gary: I like living in a nice house and a pretty neighborhood because it's easier. Easier than what? Easier than living in the ghetto. Why? Because in the ghetto, people have a defined element of what they think life is, and it's all about how they have to get their piece before somebody else does. That's an incredible level of limitation they assume is true.

Why are some people able to move out of the ghetto and why is it that other people never can? Because of the defining element of what they call life.

Call Participant: If you are living in a nice neighborhood, is that also a limitation of some sort?

Gary: It doesn't have to be. But living in the ghetto doesn't have to be either.

I know a lady who lives on about a hundred acres. She goes out and sits on her porch and listens to the birds and the wind chimes and enjoys what she calls that her beautiful life. That and her horses are the sum total of her life. She doesn't go outside the realm of comfort she has defined as the life she always wanted to have.

Dain: Let me give you another example.

Dain: When I was a kid living in the ghetto, there was a lady who was my source of hope. She was the mother of a friend of mine. She was a kind, caring, beautiful woman. She lived in the ghetto, but the ghetto didn't live in her. I would go to her house after school.

I was experiencing some horrendous abuse at the house where I lived. For example, I wasn't allowed to eat. What little kid is not allowed to eat in his own house? So I would go to my friend's house after school and his mom would feed me homemade tortillas and tell me that everything was going to be okay.

When you are actually *living*, there is the defining element of life, and there is the demand that you're going to live no matter what's around you. That's the difference. This lady was an example of that. She helped me get through living there. I don't know if I would have survived without her being there.

Gary: Great example, Dain. How many of you have defined what your life should be if you were having the life you would like to have? And are you trying make your choices based on the definition of the life you have decided you would like to have, which has nothing to do with what is actually going on in the world or in your life?

LIVING

Let's go on to *living*. *Living* is the action one takes in every moment of every day. The point of view of the lady who has the horses and the hundred acres is that she has the life she always wanted. Her idea of living is to go off of her ranch to do certain things that are not part of the ranch. She calls that her "living time."

> What have you defined as your "living time"? Everything that is times a godzillion, will you destroy and uncreate it all? Right and Wrong, Good and Bad, POD and POC, All 9, Shorts, Boys and Beyonds.

You guys have a lot of definitions about your living time. And your time for living. I see people create the definition "When I retire, then I can live. I can do everything I really like to do." For them, living begins when retirement occurs. Is that really going to create the living you want? Or is there something else that is possible?

> What physical actualization of the terminal and equivocal disease of choice, question, possibility, and contribution are you not acknowledging as the determining factors of living according to the rules of living on planet Earth? Everything that is times a godzillion, will you destroy and uncreate it all? Right and Wrong, Good and Bad, POD and POC, All 9, Shorts, Boys and Beyonds.

Dain:
> What physical actualization of the terminal and equivocal disease of choice, question, possibility, and contribution are you not

acknowledging as the determining factors of living according to the rules of living on planet Earth? Everything that is times a godzillion, will you destroy and uncreate it all? Right and Wrong, Good and Bad, POD and POC, All 9, Shorts, Boys and Beyonds.

Call Participant: The determining factors of living on planet Earth—could you please go into that?

Gary: Everybody is trying to tell you how you are supposed to live. To live equals what, on planet Earth? It doesn't equal the actualization of choice, question, or possibility. It is never about living from the question. It is always about living from the answer. That is the limitation that we try to function from. We say, "If I just get the right answer, if I just get this, I will have the life I want, and I will live the way I want."

Choosing to live the way you would really like to live is a totally different universe.

Call Participant: Please go into that.

Gary: *Life* is about the accomplishment. Living is what you do to accomplish the results you desire to have.

There is a guy I buy gold items from. He called me today and said, "Are you in town? I've got some good stuff."

I said, "Well, not until the 17th. Can you hold it?

He said, "I need some money."

I've spent a lot of money with him in the last few months, and I know that he has had more cash available to him now than any other time in his life. I am the primary source for what he sells. And for some reason, he was hysterical about the fact that I wasn't in town to buy from him. He has to find another way of dealing with things, but instead of doing that, he started to go for the life he wanted. He got a trophy wife, so he has someone who will cook and clean and take care of him. He also has created the idea that now he is selling a lot of things to me, he can live. So he is living higher than he has in a long time, and he still considers it less than living the way he knows he should. Would you run that process again, Dr. Dain?

Dain:

What physical actualization of the terminal and equivocal disease of choice, question, possibility, and contribution are you not acknowledging as the determining factors of living according to the rules of living on planet Earth? Everything that is times a godzillion, will you destroy and uncreate it all? Right and Wrong, Good and Bad, POD and POC, All 9, Shorts, Boys and Beyonds.

Call Participant: Are life and living both distractor implants?

Gary: Yes, they are both distractors because they distract you from generation, creation, and institution, and they distract you from choice, question, and possibility.

Dain: Which is why there are so few people who believe they have choice in anything. In essence, it is as if we have no choice. It's as though we live in a choice-less universe, even though choice is our most dynamic capacity.

Call Participant: Are you saying that in choice there is no life and living?

Gary: In choice, there is a constant generation and creation.

Dain: And in choice, there is no conclusion. There is no concluded point of view about what can be. There's only the choice and the possibilities that could be, based on the question of what could be a contribution to something different.

Death

Call Participant: That kind of ties into death and dying, too, because of completion.

Gary: That is the idea. There is completion and then death occurs. Here is something you have to get:

- The purpose of all questions is to create awareness—to have more awareness.
- The purpose of all choices is to gain awareness.

- Choice is the possibility to gain awareness of what can actually occur.
- Generation and creation are about looking at the choices, the possibility, and the energy that is going to be in existence as a result of what you choose.

Call Participant: So when people say, "The only thing you can rely on is death and taxes," it's like saying you're born to die. You are born in a distractor implant.

Gary: That is the rule of life. Here on planet Earth, life is from birth until death. That is considered the life cycle. That is how you get into this. Death becomes the end of the cycle of the action of living. You live to die.

Call Participant: No one questions that.

Gary: No, it is unquestionable. It's the thing that everybody assumes is a given. The given is that you're going to live and you're going to die. Those are the givens of life and living on planet Earth. This is the rule of living and the definition of life. You have defined the limitation of life, which is that you live and have a life until you die. And the rule of living, which is you live until you die. So death becomes the next distractor. How much energy is used to avoid death on the planet Earth? A lot, a little, or megatons?

Participants: Megatons!

Gary:
> Everything you have done to avoid that, will you destroy and uncreate it all? Right and Wrong, Good and Bad, POD and POC, All 9, Shorts, Boys and Beyonds.

Participants: Why isn't aging a distractor implant?

Gary: It's a part of living. You have to get old ... and die.

Call Participant: Oh!

Dain: A few things about death: One is that there is such resistance to it here. And anything you resist, you create with more intensity. Many people are resisting death, while at the same time creating it with all of the non-choice and non-living they are functioning from. They are choosing death while resisting it. They're locking it in, in both directions.

Call Participant: What is equivocal disease? Can you talk more about that?

Gary: When you start to do something that actually works for you, do you equivocate about it, or do you instantly know that is what you have? You equivocate. You equivocate about what you can choose, as though if you choose wrongly, you won't be living; you will be dying. I'm choosing to take eight million bottles of supplements because that is choosing to live. Is it? Or is that one man's answer of what it is? Does that help?

Call Participant: Yes. It is so insidious. It gets on you. It's almost like the opposite of resisting it is having it get on you. Aging and dying and all of that seem equivocal. It's like you go into doubt about indefinite life as a possibility.

Gary:
> What physical actualization of the terminal and totally corrosive and corrupting disease of indefinite life and living are you not acknowledging as the destructive element of death as the only choice of your reality? Everything that is times a godzillion, will you destroy and uncreate it all, please? Right and Wrong, Good and Bad, POD and POC, All 9, Shorts, Boys and Beyonds.

Dain:
> What physical actualization of the terminal and totally corrosive and corrupting disease of indefinite life and living are you not acknowledging as the destructive element of death as the only choice of your reality? Everything that is times a godzillion, will you destroy and uncreate it all, please? Right and Wrong, Good and Bad, POD and POC, All 9, Shorts, Boys and Beyonds.

Call Participant: Gary, can I be the devil's advocate? It seems that it's not so much buying that death and dying are this reality. It's more like the destructive element is resisting death and dying and pretending they are not there.

Gary: Well, yes, that would be true if you weren't trying to create death as a reality.

Call Participant: But what if you're ignoring it? It's there, but you're ignoring it.

Gary: That is still seeing it as a reality, by pretending it doesn't exist.

Call Participant: It's like the man behind the curtain?

Gary: Yeah, there is no one behind the curtain. There is no one behind the curtain, but you still believe that he is there.

Reality

Let's go on to reality.

> What constitutes reality on planet Earth? Everything, every energy that brought up, will you destroy and uncreate it all? Right and Wrong, Good and Bad, POD and POC, All 9, Shorts, Boys and Beyonds.

How many of you believe there has to be a balance on planet Earth? A balance of life and death, a balance of positive and negative, a balance of power? There isn't. That is a reality that is perpetrated on you. It keeps you in a constant state of judgment, in particular, a judgment of the wrongness of you.

> Everything you have done to buy this balance as a reality, will you destroy and uncreate it all? Right and Wrong, Good and Bad, POD and POC, All 9, Shorts, Boys and Beyonds.

When you look at a molecule, you see positive and negative electrons surround the center, which is the nucleus of the element. They are the source of what creates movement within the structure of the system of the molecule.

If you look at you as the nucleus of the molecule and you're within the molecule of your own reality, you would recognize that every time you go to wrongness, that is the moment you need to go to the strength of the positive element called change. Wrongness is the negative element. Change is the positive element. And so you create movement.

Every molecule has motion, and you have to create the motion in your life, which becomes life, which takes that motion as real living. When you are in motion, you are living. But we have defined living as "What do we have to do? What do we have to get done? What do we do outside of the places where we have to do what we institute?"

True living is motion. Total motion. Do you recognize that you are seldom comfortable being quiet? You're seldom comfortable not having something going on at all times. Why? Because there is a different possibility in motion.

> What physical actualization of the totally limiting and conceptual structuring disease of true change, are you not acknowledging as the perfection of the pathetic and piss-wad life, living, death, and reality you are choosing? Everything that is times a godzillion, will you destroy and uncreate it all? Right and Wrong, Good and Bad, POD and POC, All 9, Shorts, Boys and Beyonds.

Dain:

> What physical actualization of the totally limiting and conceptual structuring disease of true motion, motility, and explosive catalytic contribution are you not acknowledging as the perception of the pathetic and piss-wad life, living, death, and reality you are choosing? Everything that is times a godzillion, will you destroy and uncreate it all? Right and Wrong, Good and Bad, POD and POC, All 9, Shorts, Boys and Beyonds.

Gary: Ouch! Let's do it again.

Dain:

> What physical actualization of the totally limiting and conceptual structuring disease of true motion, motility, and explosive catalytic contribution are you not acknowledging as the perception of the pathetic and piss-wad life, living, death, and reality you are choosing? Everything that is times a godzillion, will you destroy and uncreate it all? Right and Wrong, Good and Bad, POD and POC, All 9, Shorts, Boys and Beyonds.

Call Participant: Can we talk some more about generative type statements instead of these statements about how horrible we are and what a crappy job we are doing in our lives?

Gary: I didn't say that.

Call Participant: Can we destroy the crappy stuff first?

Gary: How often do you say how wonderful your life is and how often do you talk about the crap in it?

Call Participant: Well, I don't have much crap, so I don't talk about crap that often.

Gary: Do your friends talk about that crap all the time? Yes, they do. People are always talking about the crap. People are always talking about the worst part of their life. They are never talking about the best part of their life. They will put more time and attention on the bad things than they will on the good things.

Call Participant: Well, that would be a yes. I agree that is often the case. But it's not so for everybody.

Gary: I am trying to get rid of the frigging distractor implants. I am not trying to make this look good for you. I want to get rid of the shit that is mucking up people's lives. *Then* we get to the other part, but we have to get through this first.

Dain: The other part of this is that when you destroy limitation, what is unlimited automatically starts to show up in your life. There are places where this functions, even though you don't get it cognitively. You're going to the place of judging that what's going on here is a wrongness, or that it's a limited point of view, or that there is some other way of going about it. There is something in this that applies to you; otherwise, there would be no charge about it.

It could be a place in your world where you're saying, "You know what, damn it? I am so tired of the world not being creative and generative!" You might acknowledge that you are making a demand for more creation and generation. If there is a charge on it, then it is having an effect on your life somewhere, and running the process, even through the charge, will change it.

Call Participant: Got it. In other words, I am resisting it somewhat.

Dain: Yes, something like that.

Call Participant: Okay, I got it. This is why we talk about the bad things.

Gary: If you don't talk about the bad things, you won't have anything to talk about, because that is what most people want to talk about.

Dain:
> What physical actualization of the totally limiting and conceptual structuring disease of true motion, motility, and explosive catalytic contribution are you not acknowledging as the perception and purchase of the pathetic and piss-wad life, living, death, and reality you are choosing? Everything that is times a godzillion, will you destroy and uncreate it all please? Right and Wrong, Good and Bad, POD and POC, All 9, Shorts, Boys and Beyonds.

Gary: One more time, Dain.

Dain:
> What physical actualization of the totally limiting and, conceptual structuring disease of true motion, motility, and explosive catalytic contribution are you not acknowledging as the perception and purchase of the pathetic and piss-wad, life, living, death, and reality you are choosing? Everything that is times a godzillion, will you destroy and uncreate it all, please? Right and Wrong, Good and Bad, POD and POC, All 9, Shorts, Boys and Beyonds.

Call Participant: At the beginning of this process, you said that wrongness is the negative and change is the positive, and motion is real living. Could you expand on that for me, please?

Gary: Every electron moves and creates a motion, which is what functions as the element of the structure. It's functions as the structure of what is actually possible in life.

As soon as you get that you're looking at the wrongness, if you will ask: "What change is available here that I haven't anticipated?" and take care of that, a different possibility can occur.

Dain: This is huge. I think you're saying that change is a creative and generative place to be. I just brought this up in the level 2 class I did in Melbourne. That one thing changed so much for people. We went through so much change on day one, and people came into day two solid as a rock, because they had so much change, which was the polarity of the positive side. But then they had to create that much wrongness to balance it out, which is why you keep going from change to wrongness.

You change, and then you go into "I am wrong" rather than asking: "What change is actually available here?" This question takes you out of—and is literally the antidote to—wrongness. Ask: "What change is actually available here?" and know that when you feel the most wrong is when the most change is available.

Call Participant: "What change is actually available here?" is an awesome question.

Gary: Yes. "What change is actually available that I haven't chosen?"

MOTION

Dain: I just had a glimpse of the whole thing about positive and negative creating motion. It is never about getting stuck only in the positive and avoiding the negative. It is about creating motion.

Gary: In 2012, as we got closer to the "cataclysm of the end of the Mayan calendar," people were trying to slow things down. The amount of slowness that was occurring in the world was mind boggling to me. I saw people going slower, and slower, and slower. Where are you, people? I didn't get what is going on. They seemed to think that one thing was occurring and I felt different possibilities. What would it take to create the constant state of different possibilities instead of buying into one way something has to be or "This one thing is the only change that is possible?"

Call Participant: If there is no balance, what else is there?

Gary: Motion! Motion!

Call Participant: Is motion the answer to balance or the answer to wrongness?

Gary: Would a being be in a constant state of rest?

Call Participant: Never.

Gary: Would a being be in a constant state of motion?

Call Participant: Yes.

Gary: When you are resting, you use your mind to create a sense of motion.

Call Participant: Yes.

Gary: In truth, your whole reality is in a constant state of motion. When you look out in nature, you see that nothing ever stays totally silent or still. If you go for a walk and you look closely, you will see thousands of bugs and things moving and all kinds of stuff happening. That is the "different." Why is it different? Because it is always a constant state of motion that occurs. There is no such thing as a body at rest. There is no such thing in the universe. You keep trying to create a sense that there has to be a positive and negative, and there has to be rest and there has to be movement. Movement and motion are not necessarily the same thing.

Call Participant: So wrongness would be a stillness or stagnancy?

Gary: Wrongness is how you try to make a stillness. It's the way you try to solidify things from this conceptual reality. You try to bring them into solidity. That means nothing is occurring.

When you know you're wrong, you are always trying to prove that you aren't going to do it, couldn't do it, didn't want to do it, or don't want to do it. You try to make yourself stop.

Call Participant: That is where I am going into the balance of everything. Balancing the motion with the stop. Oh Gary, I love you. I was just feeling that we should have motion and rest.

Gary: If we look at the molecular structure of anything, we see that the positive and negative structures are in a constant state of motion; otherwise, that thing doesn't exist in the same form. It could catalyze as something else and change its form, but it cannot maintain its form without the electrical motion of the positive and negative electrons. There always has to be motion in everything.

Call Participant: Gary, even in balance, even if you're on a tight rope or stilts, you're constantly moving. That is what happens. Have we misidentified balance?

Gary: We have misidentified that those things are balancing. They're not balancing; there is a motion that counteracts the different things that are going on around you. You're not balancing anything. You're moving in order to create! In order to create, you are in a constant state of motion, and as beings, we are way more creative than we give ourselves credit for. This constant state of trying to balance is the constant state of believing there is such a thing as balance. No, there is a constant state of motion in which you do not win, in which we either create or destroy from that movement.

We can create and we can destroy. Destruction is not such a bad thing. The problem is that we keep saying destruction is bad. Destruction is just change in which two things come together in a particular order in such a violent, eruptive, catalytic way that a new substance begins to exist.

Call Participant: And destruction is not the same as wrongness. Wrongness is stagnant. Destruction is still a motion?

Gary: Wrongness is how we try to stagnate things.

We are about as cooked as we can get here. But I do have a process that I would like all of you to run for yourselves as much as you can. Please put it on a loop so you can listen to it nonstop for the next 365 years. That's my contribution today.

Participants: (Laughing)

Call Participant: That is a short period of time.

Gary: Yes, the 365 Year Process.

> What physical actualization of the generative, creative, capacities for freedom from all distractor implants are you now capable of generating, creating, and instituting? Everything that does not allow that to occur times a godzillion, will you destroy and uncreate it all? Right and Wrong, Good and Bad, POD and POC, All 9, Shorts, Boys and Beyonds.

That is a good one.

Participants: (Cheering) Yeah, that is a nice one!

Gary:
> What physical actualization of the generative, creative, capacities for freedom from all distractor implants are you now capable of generating, creating, and instituting and everything that does not allow that to show up times a godzillion, will you destroy and uncreate it all? Right and Wrong, Good and Bad, POD and POC, All 9, Shorts, Boys and Beyonds.

Call Participant: Can you talk about what change is now available?

Gary: If you do not function from distractor implants, you can get clear on how distractor implants have been used as a weapon to stagnate you in one form or another. They try to create the sense that you must live by conceptual reality here on planet Earth. But it isn't necessary to live according to the conceptual realities of planet Earth. It's necessary for you to be the source of motion that changes all of it.

Gary:
> What physical actualization of the generative, creative, capacities for freedom from all distractor implants are you now capable of generating, creating, and instituting? *Total* freedom from all distractor implants. Everything that is times a godzillion, will you destroy and uncreate it all? Right and Wrong, Good and Bad, POD and POC, All 9, Shorts, Boys and Beyonds.

Call Participant: From your perspective, is there anything that is not immutable on this level that we call physical reality? Or can absolutely everything be changed?

Gary: Everything can be changed.

Call Participant: Thank you.

You Can Buy Into Them— or You Can Buy Out of Them

Gary: That is my perspective. When I was first given this information about the distractor implants, I would look at something and say, "That is a distractor implant. Never mind, I am not going to do that."

I didn't go into why they were distractor implants or how they were working against me. I just knew that they weren't generating what I was interested in. I had a choice. I could either buy into them—or I could buy out of them. I bought out of them every time. Every time somebody would go into anger, rage, fear, or hate, I'd say, "That is a distractor implant. Okay, cool. What do you want me to say?"

The person would say, "What?"

I'd ask, "What do you want me to say?"

They'd ask, "What do you mean, 'What do I want you to say?'"

I'd say, "Well, you obviously have something you want from me. What is it that you are doing with it?"

They'd ask, "What?" Then it would all break apart.

When they were doing blame, shame, regret, and guilt, I'd say, "I am to blame."

They'd say, "But... but..."

I'd say, "I am to blame."

They'd say, "No, that is not what I meant."

I'd ask, "Okay, so what did you mean?"

They could never explain it.

I began to look at these different elements and at how distractor implants are what they are. When other people would do them, I would use acknowledgement. I'd say, "Yes, I am bad, yes, whatever," and I'd have no point of view about it.

Life, Living, Death, and Reality

Every time I'd have no point of view, every time I didn't get into the trauma and drama of the distractor implants, they would change. And everything would change around me, and all the people would change around me.

To me, that was way more important than playing in the games of this reality. That is why it was so clear to me that these were just distractor implants and why did I care? It was odd to find that other people could not or would not choose that.

That is why I went ahead and did this series of calls—because people have to understand distractor implants. If you start to get an understanding of this, you won't have to live your life from the limitations everyone else is functioning from.

Call Participant: Are you saying then, Gary, that whenever we recognize that we are falling into a distractor implant, we can just choose otherwise?

Gary: Yes.

Call Participant: We just say, "I am not doing that"?

Gary: "I am not doing that." Or you say, "Oh, that is a distractor implant." That would be like walking along and all of a sudden, you smell that smell. And you would say, "Eww, that is yucky."

You would ask, "Where is that coming from?" You's say, "Oh, I just stepped in dog shit. I hate it when I step in dog shit." Then you go find a hose and you spray it off. You don't get into the trauma and drama of it, which is what distractor implants are designed to do. They're designed to get you so involved in them that you can't see what is.

Dain: You wash it off and move on. You do whatever that takes.

Gary: You put yourself in motion.

Dain: A distractor implant is designed so that you step in a pile of dog poo and then you start making poo rain from the air to prove that you just stepped in poo.

Or as you try to figure out how to remove your foot from the poo, you put your other foot in it. You are trying to figure out how to get out of it instead of just moving your foot and washing it off. No. Just wash it off and move on.

You can POC and POD it or you can choose something else. Either one will work. POCing and PODing is there when you can't seem to choose something else, or when you can't seem to wash it off.

It's important to make the choice to move on. Most people, when they step in a pile of poo, never move their foot. They ask, "What kind of poo is this? Is that poo with corn? Is that poo with tomatoes? What kind of food did the dog eat?" and meanwhile the poo turns into concrete around them.

Call Participant: Gary and Dain, could you each give an example of how you agreed with someone and said, "You're right, I am to blame"?

Gary: It boils down to "I am sorry. I shouldn't have done that."

You know they are doing blame, shame, regret, and guilt and they want to go into the trauma and drama of it. They want to spend hours talking about how terrible you are. The other day, I talked to a guy, who told me that he and his wife were getting divorced. The next day, his kid called me and he said, "My parents are screaming and yelling at each other. What can I do?"

I said, "Ask them how old they are. They are acting like teenagers who have been dissed by their teenage friend. They are not actually acting like anybody who has awareness."

The kid said, "Oh."

Apparently he did it. His dad called me later and said, "Thank you so much for helping my kid. You helped all of us. I realized I have to take the high road. If my wife is blaming me for everything, then I have to go, "You're right. I am sorry."

The distractor implant is designed to distract you from what is, and in particular, it's designed to distract from what is possible.

You have to be willing to use whatever tool you have available. And you only have tools available if you don't buy into the distractor implant at all, and instead realize, "Oh, there's a distractor implant underneath what's going on here. It's a way to make me powerless and therefore to advocate the powerlessness of the person I am with." Neither of which is true.

Dain: What you said about the way it always distracts you from other possibilities is vital. In the case of anger, I have learned from Gary to lower my barriers. I have had people start to yell at me like crazy, and I just lowered my barriers to the point I was so vulnerable that I started to cry. Talk about a way to stop. They just melt.

And then I asked, "What's really going on? What's that?"

Gary: Remember that guy who called you because he thought you were after his wife?

Dain: He called me because he thought I was after his wife—and talk about anger, rage, fear, and hate being delivered. "I am going to come kill you."

I put down all my barriers and I said, "Number one, I am not after your wife. Number two, what can I do to assist you—because obviously a tough thing is going on. What can I do to help?"

He started crying on the phone. He called me later and we had an hour-long conversation. He told his wife about it, and she texted to tell me that he'd said, "That was the most amazing hour of my life. It changed more of my life than anything I have ever done in my thirty years on the planet. Tell Dain I love him."

These are the kind of possibilities we have available—the possibilities we have when we be us, when we don't let the dog poo we stepped in run us. It's when we say, "Now I am going to wash it off and choose a different possibility."

Call Participant: When you begin to step out of the distractor implant, do you become more space? Is it kind of like, "I am so much space that I don't know how to be in the space that I be right now"? Or is it "Space has always been like fun for me"?

Gary: Well, when you get to the point where you are willing to be this space and you're not willing to step back into the poo with the distractor implants, you begin to feel slightly out of synch with the rest of the world.

Call Participant: Yeah. It's almost like I am looking for the reference point of the poo.

Gary: Yes, I know, but you have to stop looking for the reference point of the poo. You've got to ask: "What choice is really here?"

When you get out of the distractor implants, you are out of synch with the rest of the world, because the rest of the world is being controlled by the distractor implants as though that is the only choice that is available.

Call Participant: Thank you very much.

Gary: This is the key to unlocking everything that has been a limitation for me.

I talked to my sister the other day for an hour, and she talked about what was good for her and what was good for her, and she didn't ask me a single question. Did she have any real interest in me? No, she had no interest in what I am doing, in what my life is. She didn't want to know any of that. She only had an interest because we are blood.

For me it was "Okay, cool, if that is what it is for you, then that is what it is for you." I don't have to have her hear me. I don't have to have an upset with her. I don't have to get her to see what I want her to see. I just allow her to have and be whatever she chooses.

When you get out of distractor implants, you stop trying to get people to see your point of view. You start letting people see where they are and to be the elements they are willing to be. You don't have any projections or expectations of them. But as long as you are doing distractor implants, you tend to do projections and expectations of others.

Call Participant: You say, "I was wrong. I am to blame," but you're still planning to keep the choice you have made. Is there anything more that is required?

You Can't Hold on to a Choice You Have Made

Gary: No, no, no. If you keep the choice you made, it's a decision. It's a judgment. When you create the choice of showing up and dealing with the other person and where they're functioning from, they start to change, then you have to change. You can't hold on to a choice you have made.

I have never held on to a choice I have made. I can choose to be angry, but it doesn't hold. Why? Because as that person begins to change, so do I. Change is the motion that eliminates the limitations and the lack of possibilities. You get to look from a different time. I don't make a choice and hold onto the choice. A choice is only good for ten seconds.

I make a choice in ten-second increments and something starts to change, and I make a new choice—because nothing remains the same. Every choice creates a different possibility. Every choice creates a different awareness. Every question creates a different possibility and a different awareness. You start to recognize that this is what you're really looking for—awareness, possibilities, questions, choice, and contribution.

Every person is a contribution to what goes on. I have gotten mad at people and gone to talk with them about the fact that I was angry or upset, and all of the sudden, it changed because I was willing to acknowledge, "Okay, I was doing a distractor implant. What is the lie here?" If you are stuck with a lie, you have to go to "I've got to change this," "This is not working," or "There is something wrong here."

It's is a whole different universe when you get that the anger is because of the lie, and once you spot the lie, the anger starts to fall apart. For instance, say you know that someone is lying to you, and you're angry because they are lying to you. Then all of a sudden, you see the lie they have been telling themselves, and your anger goes away and the choice and contribution you can be to them to create different possibilities becomes amazing. Everything changes. That makes everything work.

That is the thing with having motion. If you're in motion and you're doing it from a place of no distractors, that motion becomes a constant state of expanding possibilities, realities, universes, and everything else. It doesn't require you to limit you or contract you at all. Nor does it require you to contract somebody else.

Call Participant: So with anger, we can ask what the lie is, and that will help defuse it? And once you get that lie, you can say, "Oh okay!" and let go of the anger. Do any of the other distractor implants work that way?

Gary: With anger, you have to ask: "Is this a distractor implant or is this based on a lie?" Anger is the only one that works that way. The rest of them don't seem to work like that.

Anger is "justified" and "correct" when there's a lie—because when somebody lies to you, it creates an energy that is similar to the distractor implant. It's *similar* to the distractor implant, but it's actually very different.

Have you ever seen somebody get mad at their horse? They are beating the horse up and doing all kinds of things. In your head you can say, "That is not working. Why are you doing that?" Getting angry at a horse for something it did five minutes ago doesn't work. I worked with a lady who would ride her horse, and if he bumped a fence when he came out of the ring, she would beat the crap out of him. He had no idea why he was getting beaten. All it did was create incredible confusion.

Call Participant: Are you saying that there are two kinds of anger? There's anger that is based on a lie, which is justified. Then there is a distractor, where you're just out of control.

Gary: Yes, you're out of control, and it's designed to keep you from seeing what is. And when people don't want to see what is, even when you try to explain it to them, or show it to them, or talk to them about the lie, that is a distractor implant. You cannot show them anything under those circumstances. It doesn't work.

Distractor implants are designed to stop you. They are designed to stop you, diminish you, contract you, and make you less than you. If you buy any of it as real, you are justifying why you want to stop you, contract you, and make you limited.

I thank you all for being on this call. This has been an amazing set of calls and I hope they will create a whole lot of change for all of you.

Dain: Gary, thank you so much for these amazing processes and awarenesses. I am so grateful to have been on this call with you guys. I adore you all. You're awesome. And, what else is possible now?

Call Participant: Thank you so much for doing these calls. They're changing a lot in my life.

Participants: Thank you Gary and Dain. We love you.

Chapter Six
Fear, Doubt, Business, and Relationship

Gary: Hello everyone. Dr. Dain and I are New Zealand right now, and Dain is being interviewed on television as we speak. He'll join us later if he finishes in time.

Today we're going to talk about the distractor implants of fear, doubt, business, and relationship. The thing you have to get about distractor implants is that they are designed to keep you from looking at the power and potency you are. That is all they are designed to do: to never let you choose to be the power and the potency you are.

Fear and Doubt

Fear and doubt are just distractors. Doubt is what you do in order to stop you. In fact, anything that stops you is a distractor. You as an infinite being can be stopped how? You can't.

Call Participant: Let's say, you start to feel one of the distractor implants, fear, doubt, or whatever…

Gary: POC and POD it.

Call Participant: Do you just say, "It doesn't exist," so POC and POD it?

Gary: POC and POD it and everything that distractor implant is supposed to do. Say:

"This ain't happening to me." When you have a fear about something, POC and POD that. Then go from POCing and PODing the distractor implant to a question: "What haven't I even considered?"

Relationship

Call Participant: I have a question about relationship. We are in connection with everything, so when does that become a relationship?

Gary: *Relationship* is defined as the distance between you and another. Relationship is always about the distance between two objects. We are in relation to one another. The moon is in relationship to the sun. The sun is in relationship to the Earth. Relationship is the distance that keeps us moving around each other without actually being the communion and the connection we truly are.

When you start out in a new relationship, you look at somebody and you say, "This is the one. This is it." Which is what question? None. And from there, you go into "Now that we have a relationship, this can't be right, and something is wrong, and we need to do something different." Oh yeah, really? Are you sure?

Once you get into a relationship, once you commit to a relationship, you give up part of your point of view in order to keep the relationship, as though the relationship is the valuable product and not you. You start to cut off parts and pieces of you in order to maintain the relationship. That's what the distractor implants are specifically designed to do—to take you away from choosing you and to put you in a place where you try to choose for the relationship.

Business

Call Participant: I have been experiencing some lock down in regard to business. I just did my taxes, which brought up the awareness that I have not been willing to generate my business because I have a huge resistance and reaction to taxes and audits. I have the point of view that I don't want to make any more money, so the government can't take my money. I will beat them that way.

Gary: That's not your best choice. This is a distractor implant with business. What would it take to change it? Every time you enter in to any business deal, POC and POD all the distractor implants around it.

The purpose of knowing about distractor implants is being able to use the information to get free of them. Most of you try to buy them as real and then you try to get rid of them. No, you don't get rid of them. You look at them and say: "How much of this is a distractor implant? POC and POD all that."

People keep getting involved in these things rather than standing back and saying, "Oh, okay, there has to be a distractor implant here, because this is not working." If something isn't working with your business, it's because you're stuck in a distractor implant. Whatever part of your business is not working well, POC and POD all the distractor implants that are keeping it from being successful. You, as an infinite being, would choose to have a business that isn't working for what reason?

It's the same with your relationship. Every time you get into a relationship, POC and POD every distractor implant that is connected to it. This applies to your relationship with your children, your relationship with your business, your relationship with your parents, your relationship with everything. You have to say: "POC and POD all the distractor implants connected to this."

When I first learned about distractor implants, every time I found a distractor implant, I would say: "Okay, business, all the distractors there, POC and POD that." Then I'd ask:

- What would I like to create my business as?
- How would I like it to be created?
- What would be generative and creative?

Distractor implants are designed to get you to go into what is contractive and to step away from what is generative and creative. They are about the institution of the distractor implant reality as the sum total of what your choices are. You have to choose differently. That's all you have do—choose differently. I hope I have made that succinct enough.

Call Participant: I have noticed that there are plenty of things I could be instituting, creating, and generating with my business. It wouldn't be difficult. And those things would create more ease and greater money flows, yet I run into resistance to doing them.

Gary: That is distractor implants. You see what you could do and you either procrastinate or you don't do it at all. You, as a humanoid, do procrastination in order to prove you are strong. In the end, you come out of it and manage to accomplish everything even though you procrastinated.

Fear, doubt, business, and relationship are all designed to keep you in a place where you never choose what you truly would like to have. You are distracting yourself from desiring what you truly desire in your life. Most of you are not willing to have what you should have in your life.

> What physical actualization of the terminal and eternal disease of having everything you would like and everything you would desire are you not acknowledging as the perfection and the purchase of the distractor implants, especially of fear, doubt, business, and relationships as the sum total of choice? Everything that is times a godzillion, will you destroy and uncreate it all? Right and Wrong, Good and Bad, POD and POC, All 9, Shorts, Boys and Beyonds.

You believe that if you got everything you asked for, if you got everything you'd like to have, and if everything worked for you, life would be too easy. And if life got too easy, would it be worth living? No. That is why the distractor implant of living is what it is. You don't want to have life so easy that it takes no effort. You think that if it takes no effort, it can have no value. As long as it is difficult to achieve, you are living. In my estimation that is not quite correct.

> What physical actualization of the terminal and eternal disease of having everything you desire and you would like and everything you are not acknowledging as the perfection and the purchase of the distractor implants of fear, doubt, relationship, and business and all the rest of them as the sum total of your choice? Everything that is times a godzillion, will you destroy and uncreate it all? Right and Wrong, Good and Bad, POD and POC, All 9, Shorts, Boys and Beyonds.

Call Participant: Gary, when you say purchase, do you mean to purchase, as in buying things?

Gary: Yes, *to buy*, as in *to accept as true*. Distractor implants are not real, but you buy into them because everyone else does. You assume they must be real for you too, which isn't correct, but we keep thinking that since everybody else is doing it, we must need to purchase them as well. You don't need to purchase the distractor implants.

Call Participant: Could you please expand on what you mean when you say, "as the sum total of your choice"? Are you saying that I am using distractor implants as my choice?

Gary: You think distractor implants equal your choice. You have decided they equal your choice. It's like you try to use distractor implants to work for you—but they never do. For instance, how often do you choose a relationship that will not give you everything you will like?

Call Participant: All the time.

Gary: Yep, all the time. How often do you do business from a place that works sort of but not totally? It's not easy—there's always a problem in it.

Call Participant: I don't do that so much with the business, but I see what you're saying.

Gary: Still with business and money, do you end up in places where you have to deal with problems?

Call Participant: Absolutely.

Gary: What would it be like if you dealt with business and money from ease and not from problems?

Call Participant: So I am dealing from or choosing distractor implants?

Gary: Yes. We do this because everybody else purchases them, and since everybody else owns them, we assume that we must own them as well.

Call Participant: What would it be like not to do that? What else is there?

Gary: You have to ask:

- What else is possible?

- What else can I choose?
- <u>What would</u> I really like to work in my business?

Everybody does business or relationship from the weird place of distractor implants, and then they wonder why their business and relationship don't work. They divorce their partners or they divorce their business partners. They don't work it out, and they don't make sure that their business partner is making money, too.

Call Participant: Right.

Gary: I look at it and I ask:

- How do we make this work?
- How do we make this work for both of us?
- How do we make this greater for all of us?
- How do I make sure that these people make as much money as I do?

That is not normal. I am the boss, so nobody is supposed to make the kind of money I am supposed to make—because business is always about the guy who is in charge, the guy who's the boss. The guy who created it is supposed to get the majority of the money, and nobody else is supposed to get anywhere close to what he gets. That is not a point of view I am willing to live by.

Why? Because if I do it from the point of view that I am supposed to get everything, eventually everyone has to separate from me—because money is the greatest source of creation for the relationship of business.

Have you ever chosen a relationship, and then decided that the person didn't have enough money for you? Or have you had to pay for everything so a guy was your boy toy? Those create a place where nothing can work. You've got to be willing to look at it as it is.

Call Participant: So you come from the Kingdom of We?

Gary: Yes, exactly.

Call Participant: And I am coming from the Kingdom of Me?

Gary: Yes, you're doing the Kingdom of Me. You are trying to create a relationship that works for you with a person who can't work for you, with a person you do not see as your equal, or with a person who will not inspire you to be greater. That is what we tend to do with relationship. How many of you have chosen a relationship with someone who never inspired you to be greater but always desired you to be lesser? If you don't think that applies to you, you are one of the few miracles on the planet.

Everything that is, that is the distractor implant, folks. Will you destroy and uncreate it?

> Right and Wrong, Good and Bad, POD and POC, All 9, Shorts, Boys and Beyonds.

Call Participant: Is it possible, from your point of view, to have a relationship with somebody who is operating at all from distractor implants? Or is it something that just cannot work?

Gary: You're trying to come to conclusion right now, which is what distractor implants are designed to do—to get you to go to conclusion and contraction. You need to ask a question: "How do I work with this person?" and then you'll come to: "Oh, they are living with a distractor implant. Okay, fine. So what do I have to do?"

Can we POC and POD everything that makes them think that distractor implants are good, real and valuable? We can, but we usually don't. When I am with somebody who is angry, I POC and POD everything that allows that distractor implant. I think it in my head. What happens? It gets rid of that distractor implant. The person goes sputter…sputter…sputter…sputter—stop. That works for me. You've got to use what you know about distractor implants, not try to deal with them. You cannot deal with an implant.

You have to be with somebody who is actually available for you. And you can't have somebody available for you unless you are willing to create and generate beyond a distractor implant. It's about creation and generation. Let's run this again:

> What physical actualization of the terminal and eternal disease of having everything you desire and you would like and everything you are not acknowledging as the perfection and the purchase of the distractor implants of fear, doubt, business, and relationship and all the rest of them as the sum total of choice? Everything that is times a godzillion, will you destroy and uncreate it all? Right and Wrong, Good and Bad, POD and POC, All 9, Shorts, Boys and Beyonds.

Call Participant: If you've got something running obsessively in your mind, can you more or less assume it is a distractor implant, even if you can't fit it in to one of the headings we have?

Gary: There are things that are on automatic reverb and Mobius strips. Anything that runs through your head like that is a Mobius strip. POC and POD all the Mobius strips creating it. Do that with anything that runs obsessively, compulsively, and of course, we do have addictive, compulsive and perverted points of view...

Dain: I refer you to call number three.

Gary: Dr. Dain is off television!

Dain: I like to start my morning on TV. We ought to do more of that.

Gary: I usually do that by sitting on top of the TV. That is my way of starting my morning on TV.

> What physical actualization of the terminal and eternal disease of having everything you desire and would like are you not acknowledging as the perfection and the purchase of the distractor implants of fear, doubt, business, and relationships and all the rest of them as the sum total of true choice? Everything that is times a godzillion, will you destroy and uncreate it all? Right and Wrong, Good and Bad, POD and POC, All 9, Shorts, Boys and Beyonds.

Call Participant: You have mentioned before that abusive relationships are about cutting off parts of us, and that it's about choosing the necessity of the distractor implant. Do we lock that into our bodies?

Gary: Yes, you do. It's anything you create as a necessity instead of a choice. You guys do necessity more than choice, so you have to choose the same thing over and over again. That is why you keep trying to look for the one choice that will create all the choices. That is turning all choice into necessity; that is more important to you than having the freedom to choose anything you desire. Any time you turn a choice into a necessity, you lock it into your body, and you hurt your body with it, because necessities are typically all designed to kill your body.

> How much necessity have you locked into your body to kill your poor, sweet, little body that really doesn't want to die? Everything that is times a godzillion, will you destroy and uncreate it all? Right and Wrong, Good and Bad, POD and POC, All 9, Shorts, Boys and Beyonds.

Dain: Something has been coming up dynamically about what you just said, Gary, and it's true of all the distractor implants: We use them to not be the greatness of us. We make them real so we can fit in.

We create these necessities instead of choice to prove that we don't have any more choice and any more capacity than anybody else on this planet. We do this rather than asking: "What is different about me?" and being able and willing to be it. If we did that, everything would show up with so much ease. It is as if we won't allow ourselves to have it.

Gary: You just said something that stimulated a whole different perspective for me, Dain. I just realized that these distractor implants are designed specifically to keep us from being a leader in the world.

Dain: That is it, definitely.

Gary: You choose them because you don't want to have to step out of normal reality. You don't want to be a leader who creates a different kind of consciousness, a different kind of reality, and a different kind of planet. You would rather die in these frigging distractor implants than choose to be that kind of leader.

> Everything you have done to make that more real than a different possibility, will you destroy and uncreate all that? Right and Wrong, Good and Bad, POD and POC, All 9, Shorts, Boys and Beyonds.

Dain: The awareness about that came to me this morning as you and I were talking before the interview on TV. What I have done in the previous TV interviews was to be more, but this morning I woke up and I was complaining, "Oh I can't be it."

As we talked about it, we got that I wasn't willing to be the difference that I am. I wasn't willing to be the leader, basically. I finally got it and said, "You know what? I am going to be the leader. Whatever it looks like, I am going to be it." I realized that so much of my life I have done exactly what we were talking about: I have not been willing to be the leader, and then I saw the effect it had when I was. It's a totally different way of being in the world.

Gary:

> How many of you are using distractor implants to not be? Every distractor implant that you are using so you don't actually have to be, will you destroy and uncreate all that times a godzillion? Right and Wrong, Good and Bad, POD and POC, All 9, Shorts, Boys and Beyonds.

Call Participant: How can you step into that position?

Gary: By acknowledging that these are distractors. This is a place where you have to choose. You have to ask: "Am I willing to be the leader who creates a different reality here?"

Let's say your family has a business, and suddenly your dad dies, or the family suddenly stops the business. You will try to go to the distractor implant of "Oh my God, I doubt that I can do it" or "I am fearful I can't do it" or "I don't know how to do business" or "My business abilities are not that great" or "My relationship with my dad was what kept us in business" or "Oh, the relationship is gone now. What's going to work?" You will do an "Oh my God!" moment before you will ever ask: "What the hell am I capable of that I have never chosen?" Because you know what? There isn't one of you who doesn't have capabilities you have never looked at, chosen, or desired—ever.

> Everything that keeps you from looking at that—and that's what every distractor implant is designed to do, to keep you from looking at you—will you destroy and uncreate it all? Right and Wrong, Good and Bad, POD and POC, All 9, Shorts, Boys and Beyonds.

Dain: This thing about choice is what Gary was trying to get me to see this morning. He said about twelve different things that were designed to give me the opportunity or the possibility of simply choosing, and initially I was not willing to have that. Finally I said, "I am going to choose this no matter what! Even if I don't know how to get there, even if I don't know what it looks like, even if I don't know what it takes, I am choosing it."

It wasn't until I chose it that I got the awareness of how to institute it. That's what you have to get. There are a lot of things you're not allowing yourself to choose because you think you don't know how to get there or you don't know how to do it. You just have to choose it—and then you will find out how to get there, how to do it, and how to be it.

Gary: Every distractor implant is specifically designed to keep you from choosing to be everything you are. That's why distractor implants are so evasive, so pervasive, and so limiting in every aspect of your life. They do not inspire possibility; they only perspire limitations.

Do you want to sweat the limitations? Then keep doing the distractor implants. Do you want to inspire the possibilities? Every time you run up against one, POC and POD it and create a question.

Dain: This morning as I was getting ready to go on TV, I didn't realize that I was smack dab in the middle of whatever distractor implant I was choosing to function from—the doubt, the fear, and all that. I don't usually function from fear anymore—ever—and I didn't realize that's what was going on.

I suggest you take a note page in your iPad or get a piece of paper and write down every single one of these distractor implants. Keep it with you for the next month and whenever anything gets wonky, look over the list and POC and POD all these things.

Distractor implants stop you from having the ease, the peace, the money, the sex, and the joy you're looking for. These truly are one of the biggest things that are stopping all of that from happening.

Gary: And it's just a choice, folks. People ask, "How do I get over them?" It's not about how you get over them. It's "Why don't I look at this, realize what it really is, and stop pretending that I have no choice?" It's a pretense that you have no choice.

> What physical actualization of the terminal and eternal disease of having everything you desire and everything you would like are you not acknowledging as the perfection and the purchase of the distractor implants of fear, doubt, business, and relationships and all the rest of them as the sum total of the choice you have available? Everything that is times a godzillion, will you destroy and uncreate it all? Right and Wrong, Good and Bad, POD and POC, All 9, Shorts, Boys and Beyonds.

You use distractor implants to create your choice. It is like saying, "I can only go to McDonalds. That's the only place I am allowed to go. It's the only place I am allowed to eat, so I will go to McDonalds."

You have a whole range of gourmet possibilities, and instead you are eating at the distractor implant fast food restaurant. If you want to live as a McDonald's, it's not a problem, but if you want to go to the gourmet life and living that you could have, you might want to choose something different.

> Everything that is times a godzillion, will you destroy and uncreate it all? Right and Wrong, Good and Bad, POD and POC, All 9, Shorts, Boys and Beyonds.

Call Participant: Dain and Gary, did you each make a demand about not operating from distractor implants? What did that look like? What was that demand?

Gary: I just said, "Oh, those are distractor implants. POC and POD that. I am not buying that." All I had to do was hear that they were distractor implants and they were designed to keep me from choosing, and I said, "Nope, that is not going to work for me. I am not doing it. Period."

I made the choice. It was "I am not going to be limited by anything, especially not a frigging distractor implant." The demand I made was "I am not going to be limited by anything. I don't care what the hell is going on in the world; I am not going to be limited by it."

Dain: For me, it was twelve years ago when I said, "I am not going to live this way anymore." That opened the door. There are times when it seems easy to choose as you, to choose for you, and to choose to be you, and there are times where it feels like you just can't get there. That's where I was this morning. Gary said, "Well, you could choose this, you could choose this," and I was saying, "I can't seem to choose this." Finally, Gary asked me something like, "What are you holding yourself back from being that you truly are?"

Every time you're in one of these distractors where you can't choose to be, you are holding yourself back from being what you truly are, or you are hiding from what you truly are.

I realized that I was aware of all these other people's universes. I've got my publicist, who is a wonderful lady, and she's got her points of view about how things should be. I have friends who are wonderful people, and they all have points of view about the way things should be—and none of those points of view match the expansiveness of my reality when I am being me. I realized I was giving up my reality so I could be part of their realities.

I saw that keeping a list of the distractor implants somewhere near us, so we could refer to it continuously for a month—and POC and POD the implants every time any of them came up—would allow us to be free from them.

Call Participant: *That is a fantastic suggestion!*

Gary: More than that, more than that, you would choose to be for you.

Dain: Yeah!

Gary: I chose to be free from that. I asked: "What would it be like to not run business from the distractor implant? What would it be like to create a business that actually worked for me?" My point of view about money is that the only purpose of money is to change people's realities. So I asked, "How can I use the money that I create in my business, and how can I use my business to change people's realities? What else is important?"

Dain: Any of the things being done as they are currently done in this reality—the business-as-usual point of view—is being done from distractor implants. Business as it's currently done here on planet Earth, is being done by almost everyone from a distractor implant.

Any time we try to take a point of view about business, as an example, or about doubt, which is where I was this morning—I was doubting myself dynamically—it is based on what we have learned from the distractor implant reality around us. It is out there everywhere, and if you make the choice to go beyond it, you will find the way to go beyond it.

Call Participant: I have a question about relationship. My ex and I haven't lived together in six years. We have been intending to get divorced for quite a while, yet it has never quite happened. Is it a distractor implant that doesn't allow the marriage to actually dissolve?

Gary: Well, the marriage is already dissolved. What you're not doing is getting the legal stuff in place because it's much more convenient for both of you to say to people, "I am sorry, I can't date you. I'm still married." It's a way of keeping others out of your world. So congratulations, you have done a good job there. It's just a choice.

Call Participant: I work for my husband's family business as an admin and accountant. It's not easy when personal relationships get in the way of business or the other way around. What can we change here to have it be different?

Destroy and Uncreate Your Relationships

Gary: First of all, before you to go to work each day, destroy and uncreate all your relationships. Destroy and uncreate your relationship with your mother-in-law, with the business, and with everybody who works in it. And ask: "What can I change here to have it be totally different?"

Call Participant: I am also an Access Bars Facilitator and I work with a friend. We are aware of our judgments of each other and we are POCing and PODing them, but it is not easy for me to be her business partner.

Gary: Maybe you don't really want to be a business partner with this person. Maybe this person is not somebody who is good to be in business with. You've got to be willing to look at that. You've also got to be willing to look at what will work for you. I am always looking at "What is going to work for me? What will make it easy for me?" Note that this is not "What does it have to be?"

If you say, "Okay, that's business, it's a distractor implant," and you POC and POC it, it will be a different reality for you. If you say, "This is relationship. It's a distractor implant, POC and POD all the distractor implants connected to this," it will be a different reality. All of a sudden, you'll start to see things from a different place. But you've got to use this stuff all the time. You start there, and all of a sudden you'll get more awareness and you'll get more possibilities.

Call Participant: Is my fear of rejection, failing to succeed, and disappointing others a creation of my doubt of me, my abilities, and my capacities?

Gary: No, it is not. It is not the creation of anything at all. You are buying into the distractor implant of doubt and fear. Every time you have doubt, POC and POD all the distractor implants creating that.

That's all you've got to do, folks. You keep trying to make this difficult. You say, "I want to handle my fear." No, you don't want to handle your fear. You want to POC and POD all the distractor implants. You don't have any fear.

Dain: You can't handle something that isn't real and that you don't have. You can, however, take the easy road. Just frigging POC and POD it and don't worry about it anymore.

That's why I say:

- Make a list of all the distractor implants.
- Carry it in your pocket.
- Take it everywhere you go.
- Look at the list all the time to see whether you are doing a distractor implant. If you are, POC and POD it.

When you do this, you will start to realize that what you thought was "I am doing something wrong" is actually doubt. What you thought was this heavy thing you couldn't get over is actually fear. As you start to POC and POD the distractor implants, you will recognize them for what they are. Sometimes you have to have something go away before you can see it clearly; then you can look back and see what it actually was. Most of us have been taught that if we can figure out what it is, we can make it go away. That's putting the cart before the horse. POC and POD it, and as it goes away, you will find out what it was and you won't choose it again—unless you are having a lot of fun choosing it.

Call Participant: Doubt seems to be my favorite justification for never choosing to act. When will I start creating from any of the godzillion ideas I have? Until we started these calls, I didn't see how much I was doing this. Now it seems like doubt is everywhere in my universe. So what else is possible?

Gary: Ask: "If I give up my addiction to doubt, what other possibilities, capabilities, and other stuff I haven't even considered would be available to me?" That's the question you've got to live with, folks, because that's what is available to you if you stop buying into these things and stop choosing them.

I have a question here from a lady about her son. He's two years old and he is pushing her buttons constantly. She hates him most of the time. Anytime your kid does something that is infuriating to you, say: "I POC and POD all of the distractor implants creating this in his world and mine."

Given the fact that the boy doesn't like his head touched, it sounds like he may be slightly autistic. Autistic kids will always fight against you. You may wish to talk with Anne Maxwell. You can find her online. She can probably give you some hints about how to deal with your son more easily. But the main thing is to POC and POD all the distractors creating whatever is going on with him every day. You can also POC and POD everything your relationship was with him yesterday. Destroy and uncreate the relationship every single, solitary day so that you are starting with a clean slate each day, because both of you are functioning from these implants.

Dain: One of the things she said in her question that Gary didn't mention was "I used to be in Access and then I went away right after becoming pregnant." It might (or might not) help to ask your son, "Are you pissed off at me for stopping Access? Did you come to me to get me to do Access? And did I screw it up from your point of view by going away?"

If so, say, "I am sorry. I didn't realize I was screwing it up for you. I had my own stuff going on. How can I make up for the damage done? Will you please forgive me?" POC and POD everything in his world that is like "Dummy, I came to you so I could do Access, and then you left right before I was born. I hate you, I hate you, I hate you," which, by the way, is a distractor implant.

Gary: He may be one of the reasons you are coming back to Access now, because he wants whatever it's going to give him.

Dain: He may be frustrated and upset because you have the point of view that without his being born, you never would have gotten back on the consciousness trail. It might have been something he was trying to give you and to do for you. And it might be an invalidation of his very being that you weren't in the place to receive Access at that time.

Gary: Ask him about this when he is asleep; don't ask him when he is awake.

Dain: Yeah, ask him when he is asleep, then POC and POD it and everything you are in judgment of you about, so you can start off from a totally different place.

Gary: I hope that helps.

Call Participant: I doubt myself. I have had low self-esteem for a long time, and it has changed and improved. But there is still a situation where I become completely paralyzed and I doubt myself. How can I handle that?

Gary: Once again, you have to get that these are distractor implants! Every time you feel doubt or fear, any time you feel less-than, POC and POD all the distractor implants creating that. Please folks, make it easy on yourselves. I don't know why you like to work so hard.

to have a very similar sense of doubt, low self-esteem, y, and I can tell you that the more you POC and POD it, will change. I didn't understand how other people could ...uik around like they were totally confident and had no self-esteem issues. I never got it, until I realized that it is a choice you have.

Call Participant: I know you say fear is a lie, but I am afraid of dogs. I have POCed and PODed any energy in connection with my fear many times, but unfortunately, it does not fully help. I am still scared. This is very disabling for me. How can I change my fear of dogs?

Dain: (Speaking with intensity) Here is something I want to know: What potency are you refusing with all this crap you keep pretending is actually you, with your fear, your doubt, and your "I am so pathetic I barely deserve to breathe" point of view? What the hell are you doing? What are you perpetrating on you and the world when you pretend that is true for you? Because you are one potent being, whether you know it or not. I say that from personal experience, by the way.

Gary: (to Dain) Who the heck just showed up?

Dain: Here's what it is. I recognized it after hearing the second question about how pathetic you are pretending to be. You think it is real for you. But you've got some serious potency, my dear, no matter what your life has looked like until now. You've got some serious potency that you are twisting into the impotence you are pretending is true for you. Will you do me a favor—a personal favor—will you stop now before I come to wherever you are and kill you? Thank you!

> Everything that is times a godzillion, will you destroy and uncreate it, please? Right and Wrong, Good and Bad, POD and POC, All 9, Shorts, Boys and Beyonds.

A lot of you might recognize this as true for you as well. Run this process for the next three weeks:

> What potency am I refusing with this fear, doubt, and all the other crap I am choosing? Destroy and uncreate it all, times a godzillion. Right and Wrong, Good and Bad, POD and POC, All 9, Shorts, Boys and Beyonds.

Gary: You are scaring me, Dain! I am going to run away.

Dain: Something turned me on. I just saw that and I said, "Enough!" We do these things to ourselves so dynamically! We've got so much potency and so much capacity that we refuse to know.

Call Participant: I find myself creating on a huge scale, yet I have the viewpoint that it isn't possible. I recognize this as a doubt implant and I try to send it away. Now a new thought whispers that I am living in a fantasy by trying to create something on this large a scale.

Gary: You are. It's the fantasy world you always knew was true, that everybody else told you couldn't be. Welcome to your world. You live, and I live, in a fantasy world by other people's standards. People tell me all the time, "You can't do that." Then I do what they say can't be done, and it works.

When I arrived here in New Zealand, I went to my second most favorite antique shop in the world, and I bought a bunch of stuff for my antique shop in Brisbane. When I went to pick up everything, the owners of the store said, "We are so grateful you came in. We were about to close down. We've been in bad straits for three months and we didn't know what we were going to do. You just saved our lives." It's a different world when you save somebody's life that way. It creates a whole different set of possibilities. There is a different reality for you. It's like you live in a fantasy world that shouldn't be.

The idea it shouldn't be is the distractor implants of the McDonald's world that everybody else lives in. You live in a gourmet fantasy world in which everything you taste and everything you eat works for you. You get everything you truly desire, everything you require, and everything you want. You get it all. That's the way it's supposed to be.

Call Participant: My life is falling apart. I have been a single mom for a year now, and I like that part of it. I have my own business in the area where I live. But I feel alone and a little depressed, as I spent the last six years with my ex's friends and family. So now I'm here quite by myself and I feel stuck. I can't see how to move myself and my business. My clients will not move with me. It will be too far for them. And that is my income right now. I want to move into the city where I lived before, but the apartments there are more expensive, and it will take time to build up a clientele. Money-wise it does not look good at the moment.

Gary: I want to point something out: You didn't ask a single question. None of the things you said are questions, are they? They are all conclusions. They are all conclusions based on the fear and doubt distractor implants.

So the first thing is: There are other alternatives. Either/or are not the only choices in the world, folks. For example, you could go to the city a couple of days a week, get an office space, and start creating clientele in the new place until you have enough clients to move there.

Dain: Even if you just rented a room in someone else's office or worked out of a healing center. That's one possibility. Do it just a couple of days a week to start. If you take one step, it gives you the encouragement take another step, and then you can take another, and another. Even going to the city and looking around or looking at ads and seeing places people have for rent is doing something that will start to turn things around. And don't be discouraged if those things don't turn out well—just keep going.

Gary: You are operating from the fear, the doubt, the business, and the relationship distractor implants as well as the conclusions you have reached. All those distractor implants have you in the place where you think you don't have choice. And that's exactly what they are designed to do.

Call Participant: I have turned out not to be a person I would like to be. Many years ago, I was a happy person and I had lots of people to hang out with. Now I am defensive whenever people say the smallest thing to me.

Gary: If you are that defensive, you were in an abusive relationship. The abuse was based on the fact that you were willing to sell you to have a relationship. That is the distractor implant point of view.

> How many of you have sold yourself in your relationship? In your relationship, in business, in your relationship to your fear, and in your relationship to your doubt? Those are the sales points that purchase back into the distractor implant every time. Everything that is times a godzillion, will you destroy and uncreate it all? Right

and Wrong, Good and Bad, POD and POC, All 9, Shorts, Boys and Beyonds.

You are probably a smart person, and because you are smart and because you were happy, you assumed you could not be in an abusive relationship. Abuse happens a little bit at a time, folks. You need to listen to some of the Abuse CDs we have, and you need to get clear that there is a different possibility.

If you are defensive and you are waiting for the other shoe to drop, you have been in a defensive position brought on by an abusive relationship. You've got to clear that before you are going to get all of this information about distractor implants.

Call Participant: It sucks. I am running around in circles. I am not a victim, but I am quite confused.

Gary: That is because you lack information, and hopefully this information will start you on the process of changing all of this.

Call Participant: Gary, I was in a relationship where there was physical and verbal abuse. The tools of Access really assisted me in choosing something different. I use many of the tools, and they are clearing a lot of stuff. Recently, though, it feels like I am becoming more sensitive to people. It seems like I am overly sensitive to what they say. I did some swaps with a few different people who do metaphysical stuff, and all of them said I've got a broken heart.

Gary: Can I ask you a question?

Call Participant: Yes, please.

Gary: What question is "You have a broken heart"?

Call Participant: Yeah, I know there is no question in that.

Gary: They just gave you their answer, and now it is sticking you. If you go to metaphysical people, you are wasting your money as rapidly as you can, because all they will do is give you their answer. It's their point of view of what you have to deal with. Their point of view of what your problem and what your "issue" is. They are not interested in you becoming aware. They are interested in you buying more of their wares. How many lifetimes have you been buying the idea that you have a broken heart? And no, you are not sensitive; you are aware. What part of *aware* do you not get?

> Everything that is times a godzillion, will you destroy and uncreate it all? Right and Wrong, Good and Bad, POD and POC, All 9, Shorts, Boys and Beyonds.

You've got to start looking at this and ask: "Is that true? Do I have a broken heart?" If you had a broken heart, you'd be dead! You don't have a broken heart. You have lost your faith in relationship, but that's not a bad thing. You don't want blind faith in relationship. You want to look at what is and ask: "Is this a good person? Will he take care of me and will he love me and care for me? Does he want to be with me?" Not: "I need a good person who will love me totally, and now my heart will heal." What a crock of shit. I am sorry you've been in an abusive relationship. Does your body need to cry? Yes, your body needs to cry. Let it frigging cry. Stop trying to stop it!

Dain: Do you really have a broken heart? Or have you stepped into a huge amount of awareness? And if you called awareness what it actually is, would your body finally release this stuff it has been trying to release instead of going onto an Mobius strip based on somebody else's lie and their perpetration on you that you have a broken heart? Sorry, I'm sure you notice we are delivering this with a bit of intensity.

Call Participant: Yeah, that's fine. I want to get clear of this. I want this to change.

Dain: That is why we have this level of intensity. You gave up your knowing for somebody else's significant, concluded, metaphysical point of view that has stuck you ever since. Yes or No?

Call Participant: Um, I would say I've been in question with it.

Gary: I am sorry, but you can't be in question of it because you just delivered it as an absolute, flat-out statement of fact. That's not a question.

Call Participant: Okay, yes.

Gary: If you try to buy somebody else's lie, all you are going to do is destroy you. Please stop this. Please don't do this to you. You deserve better than this. You deserve more than this, and if you buy the idea that you have a broken heart, then you can only heal it by finding somebody else who will abuse you differently.

Dain: Ask: "Do I really have a broken heart? Have I been buying this from somebody else? And, if I stop buying this particular stuff, what else would change in my life?" And you, my dear, have way more potency than you have been wanting to acknowledge.

Gary: Forever...amen!

Dain: You keep going to people who think they have more awareness than you, and they don't have near the level of awareness you have. They don't have near the level of adventure you have. They don't have near the level of being you have. They don't have near the level of caring you have. They don't live in nearly the level of question you do.

Gary: Or the possibility.

Dain: You let them give you their limited answer and you walked off trying to make it real. And you beat you up every time it doesn't seem to work. Well, it's not going to work. You're greater than what they are telling you.

Gary: Please don't go to people who are trying to find what's wrong with you. There is nothing wrong with you.

Dain: I've got to tell you, I've done this dynamically for most of my life, and every time I've made someone else's point of view greater than me, I've always come away screwed up. I'd wonder why and try to find my way out of it. And the only way out of it was when I acknowledged, "Oh, I am greater than what this person has been telling me, and I've been buying their conclusion! No more of that shit."

Call Participant: Ok, so the best way to deal with it in my body is to cry?

Gary: Yeah, that's your body.

Call Participant: And when it comes up just cry?

Gary: POC and POD it and cry.

Dain: Let your body cry, and ask it: "Hey body, what's it going to take to dissipate this?" But it's crying not from the point of view, "I've got a broken heart," because that is a significance and a lie.

Gary: The reality is that your body was abused. You were abused. Your body received all the abuse. It needs to have some tears in order to get rid of it all.

Dain: And is it a broken heart or is it the caring that you refuse to have for you? That's what your body is desiring and requiring at this point. What we would hope for you is that you will say, "I am going to care for me, and I am going to care for my body now, and I am not going to buy other people's points of view that there is something wrong with me. Because what if there is nothing wrong with me?"

Gary: There is nothing wrong with you. There is nothing wrong with any of you, folks. None of you have anything wrong with you. But you keep buying that instead of thinking about the rightness of you.

Call Participant: Thank you.

Dain: You are welcome.

Call Participant: I realize I have applied "What if?" in the spherical sense, rather than "What's possible?" in all areas of my life. I know I bought this from my dad.

Gary: Your dad was a distractor implant looking for a place to happen. You know, just because you bought this from your dad doesn't mean you have to keep it. Just because the man was wonderful in so many respects doesn't mean he was perfect. Let go of the distractors he had. Start POCing and PODing every distractor beneath this. Ask: "What can I ask and demand to change this?" and start functioning from a totally different place.

Call Participant: How do we help people with distractor implants?

Gary: You POC and POD them. You can ask: "Are you aware this is a distractor implant? Nice, we're playing with a distractor implant."

Nobody in this reality tells you that distractor implants are not real. You can be someone who does that. You've got to be the person who's so different that you tell people what is, so they have a different choice.

Dain: We tend to fit the confines of other people's realities when we are speaking with them rather than talking about what is there and what can be cleared. We try to fit into the parameters and confines of somebody else's point of view about these things.

I want to say this, because I've seen it for all of us. In those moments, where you feel like you are the worst thing in the world, and you can't do anything, and you feel like you are the most pathetic person you've ever been, you find your way out of it and all of a sudden you have more of you than you had before.

All of you have a greater capacity to do everything from a different place. You can use this information to create your relationships. It's how you can create communion with the rest of the world.

Gary: It's how you create your life.

Dain: You can create the rest of your life. You truly have different choices available, and you have to be willing to choose those. You have to be willing to be that different, and you have to be willing to be the brilliant, shining light of a different possibility—because you can.

Gary: You can be the inspiration. I want to read something here because it sums up my point of view and I thought it was cool:

A huge gratitude, thank you, Gary and Dain, for your brilliance and knowledge and to every person on this call for your amazing contribution to this world and to my life, my living, my body, and my reality. The depth and magnitude of the change and expansion that has been occurring in my life and in the lives of others around me is phenomenal beyond words. Thank you, thank you, thank you! How does it get even better than this?

That's the way I feel about all of these calls and all of you stepping up to the possibilities that are available.

Dain: You guys are a gift. The fact of you being on this call is a huge part of how and why we've been able to go where we have.

Gary: You now have the information about what the distractor implants are and how they are designed to limit you, contract you, and make you less. Making you less is the worst thing you can do to the Earth, and the worst thing you can do to mankind. So be all of you, please!

Use what you now know about these distractor implants, so you can start being everything you are. Please stop pretending you are not as great as you really are, because that's a travesty. It's a travesty for you, for me, and the entire world.

Dain: Thank you, all.

> What physical actualization of the totally limiting and conceptual structuring disease of true change are you not acknowledging as the perfection of the pathetic and piss-wad life, living, death and reality you are choosing? And everything that is times a godzillion, will you destroy and uncreate it all? Right and Wrong, Good and Bad, Poc and Pod, All 9, Shorts, Boys and Beyonds.

The Access Consciousness® Clearing Statement

Throughout this book, we ask a lot of questions, and some of those questions might twist your head around a little bit. That's our intention. The questions we ask are designed to get your mind out of the picture so you can get to the energy of a situation.

Once the question has twisted your head around and brought up the energy of a situation, we ask if you are willing to destroy and uncreate that energy, because stuck energy is the source of barriers and limitations. Destroying and uncreating that energy will open the door to new possibilities for you. This is your opportunity to say, "Yes, I'm willing to let go of whatever is holding that limitation in place."

That will be followed by some weird-speak we call the clearing statement:

Right and Wrong, Good and Bad, POD and POC, All 9, Shorts, Boys and Beyonds®

With the clearing statement, we're going back to the energy of the limitations and barriers that have been created. We're looking at the energies that keep us from moving forward and expanding into all of the spaces we would like to go. The clearing statement is simply short-speak that addresses the energies that are creating the limitations and contractions in our life.

The more you run the clearing statement, the deeper it goes and the more layers and levels it can unlock for you. If a lot of energy comes up for you in response to a question, you may wish to repeat the process numerous times until the subject being addressed is no longer an issue for you.

You don't have to understand the words of the clearing statement for it to work because it's about the energy. However, if you're interested in knowing what the words mean, there are some brief definitions given below.

Right and Wrong, Good and Bad is shorthand for: What's right, good, perfect, and correct about this? What's wrong, mean, vicious, terrible, bad, and awful about this? The short version of these questions is: What's right and wrong, good and bad? It is the things that we consider right, good, perfect, and/or correct that stick us the most. We do not wish to let go of them since we decided that we have them right.

POD stands for the **p**oint of **d**estruction, all the ways you have been destroying yourself in order to keep whatever you're clearing in existence.

POC stands for the **p**oint of **c**reation of the thoughts, feelings, and emotions immediately preceding your decision to lock the energy in place.

Sometimes people say, "POD and POC it," which is simply shorthand for the longer statement. When you "POD and POC" something, it is like pulling the bottom card out of a house of cards. The whole thing falls down.

All 9 stands for the nine different ways you have created this item as a limitation in your life. They are the layers of thoughts, feelings, emotions, and points of view that create the limitation as solid and real.

Shorts is the short version of a much longer series of questions that include: What's meaningful about this? What's meaningless about this? What's the punishment for this? What's the reward for this?

Boys stands for energetic structures called nucleated spheres. Basically these have to do with those areas of our life where we've tried to handle something continuously with no effect. There are at least thirteen different kinds of these spheres, which are collectively called "the boys." A nucleated sphere looks like the bubbles created when you blow in one of those kids' bubble pipes that have multiple chambers. It creates a huge mass of bubbles, and when you pop one bubble, the other bubbles fill in the space.

Have you ever tried to peel the layers of an onion when you were trying to get to the core of an issue, but you could never get there? That's because it wasn't an onion; it was a nucleated sphere.

Beyonds are feelings or sensations you get that stop your heart, stop your breath, or stop your willingness to look at possibilities. Beyonds are what occur when you are in shock. We have lots of areas in our life where we freeze up. Anytime you freeze up, that's a beyond holding you captive. That's the difficulty with a beyond: it stops you from being present. The beyonds include everything that is beyond belief, reality, imagination, conception, perception, rationalization, forgiveness, as well as all the other beyonds. They are usually feelings and sensations, rarely emotions, and never thoughts.

You can access more information about the clearing statement at http://www.accessconsciousness.com/content60.asp

OTHER BOOKS BY ACCESS CONSCIOUSNESS®

Salon des Femmes
By Gary M. Douglas

Salon des Femmes is based on a series of teleclasses Gary Douglas held with a group of women. They discuss men, sex, relationships, men's and women's roles, and creating amazing, harmonious relationships. It blends ground-breaking Access Consciousness® tools and processes, insightful revelations and heart-warming inspiration.

The Gentlemen's Club
By Gary M. Douglas

These wide-ranging conversations are in turn, funny, moving, outrageous, raunchy, and profound. Douglas offers ground-breaking Access Consciousness® tools and processes, insightful revelations, and incredible information about how to talk to a woman, how to stimulate her body, how to create orgasms by expansion rather than contraction, and how to create sex and relationship from an awareness of what is rather than a fixed point of view about what they are supposed to be.

The Ten Keys to Total Freedom
By Gary M. Douglas & Dr. Dain Heer

The Ten Keys to Total Freedom are a way of living that will help you expand your capacity for consciousness so that you can have greater awareness about yourself, your life, this reality and beyond. With greater awareness you can begin creating the life you've always known was possible but haven't yet achieved. If you will actually do and be these things, you will get free in every aspect of your life.

Beyond the Utopian Ideal
By Gary M. Douglas

Most people operate from a fixed idea or concept of how things are supposed to be, rather than functioning in the moment, where they can change anything as needed to accomplish and create more. These things are not actually real; they are conceptual realities that have been dropped into our existence. This book is about becoming aware of the ideal concepts and constructs that create limitations and barriers to what is possible for you. The constructs have to come off so you can create a world that works for you.

Divorceless Relationships
By Gary M. Douglas

A Divorceless Relationship is one where you don't have to divorce any part of you in order to be in a relationship with someone else. It is a place where everyone and everything you are in a relationship with can become greater as a result of the relationship.

Being You, Changing the World
By Dr. Dain Heer

Have you always known that something COMPLETELY DIFFERENT is possible? What if you had a handbook for infinite possibilities and dynamic change to guide you? With tools and processes that actually worked and invited you to a completely different way of being? For you? And the world?

For more Access Consciousness® Books go to
www.accessconsciousnesspublishing.com

Scan for more information

Access Seminars, Workshops & Classes

If you liked what you read in this book and are interested in attending Access seminars, workshops or classes, then for a very different point of view, read on and sample a taste of what is available. These are the core classes in Access Consciousness.

The Being You, Changing the World Class
3½-Day Intensive
Facilitated exclusively by Dr. Dain Heer

What would it be like if you created a bigger life and a reality worth playing in? Are you always asking for more, and looking for that 'something' we all know is possible? What if that 'something' is YOU? What if you, being you, is all it takes to change everything; your life, everyone around you, and the world?

This 3.5 day event is designed to take you from having a life run on autopilot—into becoming FULLY ALIVE and totally present as the infinite being you truly are. It will open you up to an expanded awareness of a life without judgment and empower you to know that you *know*.

With the Access Consciousness tools, perspectives and verbal processing that these days offer, you can start changing any area of your life that isn't working for you—like relationships, money and body—and start creating the future you truly desire.

You'll also experience Dr. Dain Heer's unique transformational process called The Energetic Synthesis of Being and receive an experience of *being you* that is impossible to describe, that you won't find anywhere else and that will stay with you for the rest of your life, if you allow it!

This class has no prerequisites and every event is uniquely created by the people who choose to come. Together, we'll go on a journey of creation… to a space that has never existed before.

What if you, truly being you, is the gift and the change this world requires?

Prerequisites: None

Access Bars (one day)
Facilitated by Certified Access Bars Facilitators worldwide

Bars is one of the foundational tools of Access. In this one-day class, you will learn a hands-on energetic process, which you will gift and receive during the class. The Access Bars are 32 points on the head that when lightly touched clear all of the limitations you have about different areas of your life and body. These areas include money, aging, body, sexuality, joy, sadness, healing, creativity, awareness and control, plus many more. What would it be like to have more freedom in all of these areas?

In this one-day class you will learn the basic tools of Access Consciousness and receive and gift 2 Access Bars sessions. At worst it will feel like a great massage, and at best your whole life will change!

Prerequisites: None

Access Foundation
Facilitated by Certified Access Facilitators worldwide

After the Access Bars, this two-day class is about giving you the space to look at your life as a different possibility.

Unlock your limitations about embodiment, finances, success, relationships, family, YOU and your capacities, and much more!

Step into greater possibilities for having everything you truly desire in life as you learn tools and questions to change anything that's not working for you. You also learn a hands-on body process called Cellular Memory that works wonders on scars and pains in the body! If you could change anything in your life, what would it be?

Prerequisites: Access Bars

Access Level 1
Facilitated by Certified Access Facilitators worldwide

After Access Foundation, Level 1 is a two-day class that shows you how to be more conscious in every area of your life and gives you practical tools that allow you to continue expanding this in your day-to-day life! Create a phenomenal life filled with magic, joy and ease and clear your limitations about what is truly available for you.

Discover the 5 Elements of Intimacy, create energy flows, start laughing and celebrating living and practice a hands-on body process that has created miraculous results all over the world!

Prerequisites: Access Foundation

Access Levels 2 & 3
Facilitated Exclusively by Gary Douglas (Founder of Access Consciousness) and Dr. Dain Heer

Having completed Level 1 and opened up to more awareness of you, you start to have more choice in life and become aware of what choice truly is. This four-day class covers a huge range of areas, including the joy of business, living life for the fun of it, no fear, courage and leadership, changing the molecular structure of things, creating your body and your sexual reality, and how to stop holding on to what you want to get rid of! Is it time to start receiving the change you've been asking for?

Prerequisites: Access Bars, Foundation and Level 1

The Energetic Synthesis of Being (ESB)
3½ Day Advanced Class in Being
Facilitated Exclusively by Dr. Dain Heer

Would you like to know without a doubt that you can change anything in your life, in your body…in the world? This is one of the most advanced workshops in consciousness and energetic change currently being taught. It's a class that is totally undefined, and it recreates itself in every moment with every person…every energy…that shows up. It's a 3½-day exploration of the energy, space and consciousness that you as a being truly be, and it gives you access to the space where you can begin to play with all the energies of the universe and choose to be the totality of you, being fully alive and embodied.

A new section has been added to this class where Dain invites you to start working on other people, exploring what he calls the Energetic Symphony of Being. In this part, each of you add your knowing and your being to the ESB energy and creates something new and amazing that has never been seen in this world before. What contribution could this class be to you? What contribution could you be to this class? What change could we create in the world?

Prerequisites: Access Bars, Foundation and Levels 1, 2 & 3

Access Body Class
Facilitated by Access Body Class Facilitators worldwide

During this three-day class you will learn verbal processes and hands-on bodywork that unlock the tension, resistance, and dis-ease of the body. Do you have a talent and ability to work with bodies that you haven't yet unlocked? Are you a body worker (massage therapist, chiropractor, medical doctor, nurse) looking for a way to enhance the healing you can do for your clients? Come play with us and begin to explore how to communicate and relate to bodies, including yours, in a whole new way.

Prerequisites: Access Bars, Foundation and Level 1

About Gary M. Douglas & Dr. Dain Heer

Gary M. Douglas

The illustrious best-selling author and international speaker, Gary Douglas, pioneered a set of transformational life changing tools and processes known as Access Consciousness® over 25 years ago. These cutting edge tools have transformed the lives of thousands of people all over the world. In fact, his work has spread to 178 countries, with 2,000 trained facilitators worldwide. Simple but so effective, the tools facilitate people of all ages and backgrounds to help remove limitations holding them back from a full life.

Gary was born in Midwest USA and raised in San Diego, California. Although he came from a "normal" middle class family, he was fascinated from an early age with the human psyche and this interest grew into a desire to assist people to "know what they know" and expand into more awareness, joy and abundance.

These pragmatic tools he has developed are not only being used by celebrities, corporates and teachers but also by health professionals (psychologists, chiropractors, naturopaths) to improve the health & wellbeing of their clients.

Prior to creating Access Consciousness® Gary Douglas was a successful realtor in Santa Barbara, California and also completed a psychology degree. Although he attained material wealth and was regarded as "successful," his life began to lack meaning and so he began his search to find a new way forward—one that would create change in the world and in people's lives.

Gary is the author of 12 books including the best selling novel *The Place*. He describes the inspiration behind the writing, "I wanted to explore the possibilities for how life could be. To allow people to know there actually is no necessity to live with the ageing, insanity, stupidity, intrigue, violence, craziness, trauma and drama we live with, as though we have no choice. *The Place* is about people knowing that all things are possible. Choice is the source of creation. What if our choices can be changed in an instant? What if we could make choice more real than the decisions and stuck points we buy as real?"

Gary has an incredible level of awareness and care for all living things, "I would like people be more aware and more conscious and to realize we need to be stewards of the earth not users and abusers of the earth. If we start to see the possibilities of what we have available to us, instead of trying to create our piece of the pie, we could create a different world."

A vibrant 70-year-old grandfather (who is almost "ageless") with a very different view on life, Gary believes we are here to express our uniqueness and experience the ease and joy of living. He continues to inspire others, teaching across the world and making a massive contribution to the planet. He openly proclaims that for him, "life is just beginning."

Gary also has a wide range of personal and other business interests. These include: a passion for antiques (Gary established "The Antique Guild" in Brisbane, Australia in 2012), riding spirited stallions and breeding Costarricense De Paso horses, and an eco retreat in Costa Rica set to open in 2014.

To find out more, please visit:

www.GaryMDouglas.com

www.AccessConsciousness.com

www.Costarricense-Paso.com

Dr. Dain Heer

Dr. Dain Heer is an international speaker, author and facilitator of advanced Access Consciousness® workshops worldwide. His unique and transforming points of view on bodies, money, future, sex and relationships transcend everything currently being taught.

Dr. Heer invites and inspires people to greater conscious awareness from total allowance, caring, humor and a deep inner knowing.

Dr. Heer started work as a Network Chiropractor back in 2000 in California, USA. He came across Access Consciousness® at a point in his life when he was deeply unhappy and even planning suicide.

When none of the other modalities and techniques Dr. Heer had been studying were giving him lasting results or change, Access Consciousness® changed everything for him and his life began to expand and grow with more ease and speed than even he could have imagined possible.

Dr. Heer now travels the world facilitating classes and has developed a unique energy process for change for individuals and groups, called The Energetic Synthesis of Being. He has a completely different approach to healing by teaching people to tap into and recognize their own abilities and knowing. The energetic transformation possible is fast—and truly dynamic.

To find out more, please visit:

www.DrDainHeer.com

www.BeingYouChangingTheWorld.com

www.BeingYouClass.com

CPSIA information can be obtained
at www.ICGtesting.com
Printed in the USA
FSOW02n1059201015
12357FS